CURRY, CORDUROY AND THE CALL

CURRY, CORDUROY AND THE CALL

A Mennonite missionary's daughter grows up in rural India

Gwendolyn Hiebert Schroth

Outskirts Press, Inc.
Denver, Colorado

Outskirts Press, Inc.
http://www.outskirtspress.com

ISBN: 978-1-4327-7749-4

Outskirts Press and the "OP" logo are trademarks belonging to Outskirts Press, Inc.

PRINTED IN THE UNITED STATES OF AMERICA

This book was based on one family's experiences. Liberties have been taken with some characters. Names and identifying details of others were changed. The intent was to portray the lives of missionaries' children in the mid-1900s.

Contents

Acknowledgments

I WOULD LIKE to give a special thanks to my husband, Richard, who loves me and appreciates my work. I owe a debt of gratitude to Dr. Fred Tarpley, who has a gift for finding the good in everyone he encounters. He gave freely of his time and knowledge to make this publication possible. The book is written in honor of all of those who attended that boarding school in Kodaikanal, South India, and my classmates in particular.

Illustrations provided courtesy of Phyllis Hiebert Martens with technical support from Loey Hiebert Knapp.

Prologue

IN 1899 NICHOLAS and Susie (Wiebe) Hiebert, my grandparents, went to India and settled in the Hyderabad area now called Andhra Pradesh. These grandparents were among the first missionaries to the region. After two years, sickened by malaria, they returned to Minnesota, where Grandpa took over as minister of the local Mennonite Brethren Church.

On August 9, 1927, John Nicholas Christian Hiebert and Anna Luetta Jungas, my parents, were married. After their seminary studies in New York, they packed up their infant, Phyllis, and sailed for India, following in my grandparent's footsteps. It was 1929. My parents served three terms as missionaries but not all at the same mission station. Over the years they spent time in Wanaparthy, Shamshabad, Kalavahurthy, Mahabubnagar, and Nagarkurnool, all in the Hyderabad region. Their final return to the United States was in 1952. Their children, Grace, Helen, Paul, Betty, and Lois, were born in India. Phyllis, Gwendolyn, Joanne, and Margaret were born in the United States.

India was governed by the British Empire during most of the family's stay in India. When the British withdrew in 1947, the ruler of Hyderabad, the Nizam, tried to maintain Hyderabad as an independent state, but in 1950 the newly established, independent India invaded and annexed Hyderabad. The Nizam of Hyderabad resigned his post.

Kodaikanal School, the boarding school where much of this story takes place, is in the Palni Hills that are in the Eastern spur of the Western Ghats Mountain Range in South India in the state of Tamilnadu. The school, once called Highclerc, was established for children of missionaries but welcomed European and American children whose parents were in India for government or business purposes. Over time, the reputation of the school spread so that students traveled from such places as Thailand and Bahrain to attend high school. After India gained its independence from Great Britain, the school began to accept Indian children as well. The school is now The Kodaikanal International School.

While numerous accounts document the hardships of early missionaries in various parts of the world, little is written about their children, who, unasked, endured the sorrows as well as joys of living in a foreign country and the difficulty of being separated from parents for months at a time, a separation that was necessary for the children to obtain an education. This book offers a view of missionary life from the vantage point of one missionary's daughter.

The stories in this book are based on family experiences in India in the mid-1900s. Liberties were taken with some characters and experiences in order to portray as accurately as possible the lives of missionary children at that time.

CHAPTER 1
For Those in Peril on the Sea

"DON'T MOVE. STAY still," Dad shouts, waking me from a sleep already fitful due to the oppressive heat on the plains of south India—cooling monsoon rains are still too far off. We sleep outside to catch even the slightest breeze, escaping the stifling air inside our bungalow. My father is only a blur through the mosquito netting that drapes from a high frame over my bed and is tucked securely around me.

"Bang!" I dive under my sheet.

"Okay. It's dead." Dad motions for the servants to retrieve the nine-foot snake curled below my bed —now minus its head. He waves away the mob of Indians gathering to loudly offer their opinions on the type of snake, our good fortune at surviving, and Dad's great aim. This Mennonite missionary was certainly sent to save more than their souls!

At six years old, I have been taught to fear anything that slithers, roars, stings, or bites here on the isolated mission station outside the village of Kalavakurthy. The nearest doctor is in Hyderabad City four hours away, more than anyone other than the missionary ever travels. Having already lost one child to disease here in India, Mom's concern over our safety is her albatross.

In 1942, with World War II in full swing, all missionaries have greater fears beyond what lurks in dark places. The question on their minds is whether to remain in India and face the threat of Japanese invasion and the possibility of capture, or flee. My parents and the other Mennonite missionaries gather to argue the wisest course. Dad's cousin, Uncle John, is adamant. He and Auntie Viola will stay, "for the duration," he says although the risk to his large family is as great as it is to ours.

At home my mother is adamant. "We must stay here. Six weeks? Cross two oceans? Think of the children--the risk!" She talks of German submarines, torpedoes, and bombs.

"Anna," Dad pleads, "We must go. We can make it—it's safer in the States. Uncle John is wrong," then drops his own bomb. "The Japanese have entered Burma; they'll be here—soon. Our five daughters, for goodness sakes!" This overture is followed by words such as "captives," "torture," and then one I don't understand—"rape." Mom is silent.

At six-years-old, I don't fear the ocean, the Japanese, or the Germans. What I do dread is that faraway mountain boarding school that gobbles up my older sisters, Phyllis, Grace, Betty, and my brother, Paul, for months at a time. "Next year," I am told; next year I will be sent away too, but I know with a certainty that I will wither up and die without my mother. My sisters' remember-whens cement that knowledge.

"Remember-when the matron spanked Allie for wetting her bed? Remember-when we were caught whispering after lights out?" Then they tell of air raids and racing to hide in trenches dug into the sides of the mountain. They argue about how many minutes it took to reach the hideouts, wait, and return to classes or to their beds, time now more important than their terror. With each tale my panic grows, but I can't speak of it, not even with Joanne, my one-year-younger-than-me sister, my almost twin. The only one I tell my secrets to.

Dad prevails. "We will go," he says, "face the perils of the deep; God willing, we will make it safely home." And the talk turns to memories that I don't share, and stories of Grandma's house in Minnesota and how happy the relatives there will be to see us.

So now we wait for The Call—not from God but from the ship's captain. During the day a coolie is hired to refresh the house by throwing water on the straw mats hung over the windows; at night we settle in around a lantern on the verandah, and Dad relieves the boredom by reading to us before we stumble to beds beneath the great sky.

The wait ends when a dusty, barefooted messenger trudges the two miles from the village to hand Dad a telegram. The Call has come; we are to make our way to Bombay immediately. No mention of the date for departure or the name of the vessel. Just come, it says. Hasty, tearful goodbyes are said to the servants who share our compound. Dad relays instructions on how to "carry on the work" to the Indian preacher, who lives in better than servants' quarters next to our bungalow, and a messenger is dispatched to inform the other Mennonite missionaries that we are leaving India. Where from or when is not disclosed, not even to our cousins who are staying behind.

For two days we ride the train to Bombay, where a new waiting begins. Taking refuge in a hotel, we languish for ten days beneath the lone electric ceiling fan, anxious, hot, and bored. Fearful of missing the summons, we remain within the confines of the hotel.

Early one morning, a messenger slips Dad a note instructing our family to make our way to the docks that night after dark. At last the waiting part of the journey is over. We kneel in prayer for the last time on Indian soil, and Dad says, "We are now in God's hands."

Apprehensive missionaries and their families, several hundred in all, spill from rickshaws, taxis, and ox carts onto the docks. Silently clutching our meager belongings, we look up at the unlit but mighty ship, the *S.S. Brazil*, anchored there in the darkness. In the moonlight, the camouflaged, gray vessel is dark and dull. The United States flag is painted over, the portholes blackened, and only a few, dim running lights outline the hull.

"Came all the way from New York," an officer confides as we enter the gangplank, "stopped in Buenos Aires. While we were there, the Japanese attacked Pearl Harbor. That's when we had to get blacked out," he adds, explaining the ship's ghostly appearance.

Is this the ship that will take us across the Indian Ocean, past Africa, and on through the Atlantic to New York? Is this vessel strong enough to evade the submarines searching for prey? The torpedoes? The bombs?

I stand on the deck beside my father, watching the shoreline recede as our new home glides quietly into the perilous waters, joining a convoy bent on reaching safer shores. No fanfare, no shouts of joy, no friends to wave farewell to. Just silence. Secretly, though, I am glad that we are leaving behind any chance that that horrible boarding school will gobble me up. For this moment I can snuggle safely pressed against my father's side.

The first days at sea are glorious! My friends and I have liberty to dash madly about the ship, annoy the crew, and play deck tennis and shuffleboard. But our parents read their Bibles and lean on the railings, gazing worriedly out to sea. All portholes have been sealed shut, and blue lights burn dimly but only in the passageways. The heat is unbearable, so our Brave Captain allows us to drag our mattresses on deck to sleep in relative comfort, lulled to sleep by the constant sw-i-i-sh, sw-i-i-sh, sw-i-i-sh of the waves. In the dark, missionaries—Methodist, Lutheran, Presbyterian, Baptist, even us Mennonites—gather to plead to God by raising our voices in song. Differences are irrelevant—infant or adult baptism, salvation or good deeds the ticket to Heaven. None of these matter now. Far into the night we sing:

"Abide with me, fast falls the even-tide." God, spare our lives.

"The darkness deepens." Sighs of despair.

"When other helpers fail and comforts flee." Bargaining now, "God, if you'll let us live, I promise . . . "

"In life, in death, O Lord, Abide with me." Finally surrender. Thy will be done. Our trust is in God now—and in our Brave Captain.

Then all hell breaks loose in the form of a storm of red spots. First chicken pox, then the measles spread throughout the ship. The high fevers, whimpers, and complaints only add to our parents' increasing anxiety because the enemy now lurks even nearer, sinking other vessels in our convoy. The Brave Captain tells our parents of a battle off the coast of Ceylon, where the British fleet retreated to East Africa after the Japanese bombed two of their cruisers, the *H.M.S. Dorsetshire* and the *H.M.S. Cornwall*. He shares the rumors of a battle at Midway that involves American forces. Yet our Brave Captain stops once to rescue a handful of passengers who managed to shoulder their life jackets before their ship sank. He orders more and more lifeboat drills.

Passengers rush to their assigned stations beside the lifeboats. "Where's Dad? Paul?" my sisters ask, tugging at Mom's skirt. She simply points to where they stand with the other brave men and boys at the front of the vessel where there aren't any lifeboats—there just aren't enough.

As our convoy shrinks, our Brave Captain announces that we will proceed alone and take our chances. Yet our most immediate concern is the order to go below at night. A radioed message from a sister ship claims a light was spotted, so the hymn singing continues but must conclude after dark settles in. Then Dad must carry my sleeping body below, go back for Joanne, followed by Mom, Phyllis, Grace, Paul, and Betty. Dad carefully arranges us on the floor with our faces pointed toward the one small vent that gives a smidgen of relief from the stale cabin air, the porthole being sealed shut. Once through the Indian Ocean, we make our one and only stop—at Capetown. But a terrible storm is raging.

"I have to get a decent cup of coffee," Mom says and goes ashore despite warnings that the ship's tossing and twisting could break the ropes that secure it to the dock. What Dad knows, but doesn't share, is that he will humor her every whim because she is carrying inside her our next sister who is not ready yet to come into this terrifying world.

Slowly and safely, we navigate the immense waters of the Atlantic. Six weeks have passed since we were smuggled aboard in Bombay, when I stand on deck with my father one evening, watching New York City's dark skyline emerge in the dusk. Not a flicker of light, just dark ghosts of buildings, yet unmistakably New York City. Planes circle overhead, protecting us through the long night. That evening's hymn is sung tearfully and gratefully:

"Now thank we all, our God, With heart and hands and voices.
Who wonderous things has done, in whom this world rejoices,
Who from our mothers' arms has blessed us on our way."

At daylight, we tromp down the gang plank. We are home; God has been good to us. Next stop? Grandma's house in Minnesota, a place where the war will exist only in the papers, on the radio, and in lengthy discussions.

"We'll go back," Dad promises before we even reach Grandma's front door. "Just as soon as God calls us. Shouldn't be long."

CHAPTER 2
In the Beginning

"WHY?" I ASK myself at six-years-old and at twelve and even beyond. Why did we have to go to India in the first place, risk our lives returning, only to rush back at the first possible moment? Why live where the water must be boiled before drinking, go without electricity or running water, drive four hours to the nearest doctor, and fight off snakes and scorpions? Why must our relatives worry about whether or not we have sunk to the bottom of an ocean or been eaten by tigers, relatives who care for us when we return every seven years or so to replenish our supplies for another term? Why The Call? Why so many goodbyes?

I stomp my foot and ask my sisters, "Did you hear a Call? I never did."

"Oooh! I'm telling. You better hope God didn't hear that." Icicles could drip from their upturned noses. So I conjure up an answer I finally can twist my mind around, an answer that comes from the past.

One oft-told family story is how, in the early 1900s, Dad's parents made a supreme sacrifice by trekking to India as the first missionaries to the Hyderabad region where white folks were so rare that gawking mobs became permanent attachments. But, after several years, riddled with malaria and having buried one infant on Indian soil, they retreated to Minnesota, where, illness or not, they managed to bring forth a dozen interesting, yet sometimes unusual, children. Even in Minnesota Grandpa found enough unsaved and even saved souls to burden with guilt, giving him leeway to pawn the farming and its ensuing poverty onto his children. Their only recourse was to scatter. Now our family has enough aunties, uncles, and cousins to make it possible for us to hopscotch across the country almost for free if we hit a few Mennonite watering holes in between.

We can visit Uncle Alvin in California, who is paid to sit and think and tells how his car went missing from his garage only to be located in the parking lot at work with the motor still running. Uncle Sam is who-knows-where, fighting for God and country. Somewhere out West is Aunt Annie, who graciously opened her home to us and calmly increased the order when we cried, "More," as we greedily drank all the white stuff that comes in picture-painted cardboard cartons, delivered right to the door. This milk certainly doesn't come from buffaloes. Then there is Uncle Harry, who, many years later, will scream, "And the dead shall rise" at Dad's funeral, riveting our attention on the corpse, almost expecting an immediate resurrection.

Uncle Clyde in New York is special because he met our boat during the war and brought gifts to the hospital for my sister, Joanne, who was dying of pneumonia, but didn't. The twins, Lando and Waldo, hold down the country right there in the middle of Kansas, providing a convenient stopover for any relative. Aunt Marie and Uncle Gus offer refuge at a North Dakota pig farm. The rest take residence in between. We will never get to know Uncle Albert, who, at the age of twelve, went fishing one warm Minnesota afternoon with his grandfather. We are told that that grandfather's cries could be heard a mile away as he carried Albert's drowned body home in the back of his wagon.

While Dad's family scattered to the winds, Mother's did not. Her mother, by virtue of her 300 pounds, never leaves her home above Grandpa's store, the backbone of that small Minnesota town. By birth or virtue of adoption or sympathy, she raised nine children, but their horizons stop right at the edge of town. And therein is the rub.

This family gathers frequently. Uncle John brings gallons of ice cream. Aunt Mable brings her chocolate layer cake, an offering in exchange for an ear to recitals of her endless illnesses or latest surgery. Uncle Lando says, "Did you hear the one about . . . ," his large belly jiggling in rhythm with his laughter. Those relatives who must travel farther—all of 15 or 16 miles—relate the latest news, mostly deaths, from their communities to which others comment, "Oh, I didn't know," or "Was the passing easy?" Yet these get-togethers are my security blanket—warm, solid, and comforting. This place is where I can come back to should I be forgotten in a train station, a ship, or distant mountain top by my zealous parents.

So, why am I recounting all this? Because there was that day, the ninth of August in 1927, when these two such diverse families—the Hieberts—Dad's family, and Mom's—the Jungases—were joined. As the story goes, Mom fell in love with a serious, young, aspiring minister, and he with the town's beauty and daughter of a wealthy businessman. So as not to risk the ire of a single church member or business patron, the entire community was invited to the wedding, which was held in Grandpa Jungas' newly rebuilt hardware store, the largest building in town.

An interesting affair that must have been, the assorted relatives eyeing one another, and the community wondering how those Hieberts with their poverty and wanderlust and those stayathome Jungases could ever be joined. What most likely happened at that wedding was this.

The Hieberts on one side were stiff, even stern, Uncle Alvin calculating the amount of flour it took to make that enormous cake; Uncle Clyde figuring his chances of being invited along on the honeymoon to the great Niagara Falls; Grandma Hiebert doubting if this bit of a bride could manage the inevitable large family to come; and Grandpa Hiebert looking distant and walking about muttering prayers. On the other side was the Jungas clan, laughing, slapping each other on the back, hugging—even kissing—while the uncles discussed profits and losses and worked the crowd to drum up interest in building a community hospital.

But the differences were soon resolved, at least between Mom and Dad. Dad always tells one story about The Call and Mom another. But I believe deep down in my heart that the real story is that, kneeling for their ritual evening prayers one night, Mom silently prayed to be delivered from the holy severity of her husband's family while Dad, right beside her, quietly beseeched God to rescue him from the rapidly closing-in clutches of her relatives. I'm sure it was right then and there that a voice from heaven above boomed, "GO TO INDIA!"

You see, as they say in church, "God always answers prayer."

CHAPTER 3
The Journey

SO THAT IS how it all began—Mom and Dad, on their knees. They were good Mennonites, not the kind who wear caps and lengthy clothing, but worthy, nevertheless, because they don't swear, dance, smoke, or go to war. They can even hide fairly easily in a crowd of Methodists and Presbyterians. Heeding The Call, they dutifully rushed off to India and returned with more children than they left with, although one remained behind buried in the warm Indian soil. Over the next few years, while Mom and Dad were preoccupied with either missionarying or preparing to missionary, they, along with a foolishly sleepy world, paid little attention to the wolf in sheep's clothing who was slyly making grand plans to take over the world. Although Hitler opened concentration camps, burned "unGerman" books by the millions, began his crazed campaigns to rid the world of Jews, and claimed that his goal was to peacefully create more living space for Germany, my parents and the rest of the world went blissfully about their business. This madman, though, would impact me and my family much as an underwater earthquake at one end of the globe creates a tsunami that travels silently to wreak havoc on unsuspecting victims oceans away.

1936—I make my entrance into the world in Salem, Oregon. This same year Girl Scout cookies make their debut, the first Social Security checks are mailed out, the Oakland Bay Bridge is opened, the Yankees win the World Series, and the Olympics are gloriously held in Berlin.

1937—Hitler's far away war on Austria and Czechoslovakia has begun. In Oregon my sister Joanne is born—the seventh child and sixth daughter. Hitler will change our lives temporarily; Joanne will change my life forever. Our family lives in a little white house, cramped quarters for Phyllis, Grace, Paul, Betty, me, and baby Joanne, who battles me for Mama's lap. (Margaret and Lois will arrive much later.)

The too-small house problem is solved when once again The Call comes to the rescue. "Return to the mission field," is what Dad hears. How, I don't know. The phone doesn't ring, and I see no letter in the mail. This Call, nevertheless, supersedes all we are doing or want to do. Otherwise made plans stop, and great turmoil ensues. Phyllis and Grace are old enough at eight and nine to help the Church Ladies and Mom pack when they are not washing diapers, cooking, and cleaning. Paul is a boy—he's exempt. Betty and I just get in the way; Joanne smiles and drools. Dad, now happily preoccupied, contacts the mission board, scurries about applying for passports and visas, and searches for supplies to tide us over the next seven years—clothing, shoes, dishes, and everything else on Mama's list.

We dash to Minnesota to say goodbye to Grandma and take one last family photo with all the aunts and uncles. Grandma and Grandpa are seated appropriately in front, and I am smugly pleased to be picked for once to be held in Dad's arms; he is just pleased as punch to be returning to India. He says, "We must go before it is Too Late." If you pay attention in church, you know what "Too Late" means.

1938—Katherine Ann Porter's *Ship of Fools* is blissfully making its way from Mexico back to the Fatherland with a cargo of head-in-the-sand idiots who ignore the fact that Hitler has taken Austria, Mussolini's name has became a household word, and the Munich Agreement has cleverly given Sudetenland to Germany without a shot. In a distant ocean, the Japanese freighter, *Hiye Maru* takes us to Japan where we transfer to the *Tango Maru* which carries our family the rest of the journey to India.

Mother takes no chances on this trip. On their previous voyage to

India, before I was born, Mom and Dad had to park Phyllis and Grace in the stateroom, charged with the care of baby Paul. British protocol allowed children to eat at 5:00 o'clock but adults only at 7:00 when they could eat in style, no muss, no fuss. The first day Mother gobbled down her food and rushed back to the stateroom, almost too late. Phyllis and Grace were holding baby Paul half in and half out of the porthole. "He wants to see the waves," they said. After that Mom and Dad took turns in the dining room.

The result of that horror is that Joanne and I are attached to leashes and tethered to Mother's arm or placed in a playpen on deck under her watchful eye. Even when we are in port, Mom and Dad keep us close because there was that voyage where Betty was lost in China, letting go of Mother's hand while she was debating the price of a colorful jacket. Mom and Dad almost had to grab their belongings and take up residence in China and save souls there until Betty was found. But, just as the ship's horn blasted its last warning for all to get on board, an American family turned up with Lost Betty, saying that they had found her wandering the streets.

The best times on this ship are when Dad lets me stand beside him at the railing to watch for leaping fish and to see the ship's pointed bow rise and fall as it forges through the sparkling water. We listen to the swish of the foam-filled waves rushing past, the white spray occasionally wetting our faces with salt. For brief moments, I am warm and safe here beside my dad.

But that safety doesn't last. A Level Five typhoon confines us to our stateroom where we can only crouch in fear in our bunks and watch our luggage slide back and forth across the floor. Mom and Dad pray loudly for our safety. The seas calm and the captain determines that the damage to the ship, although extensive, will not deter us from limping the remaining distance to a Japanese port for repairs. So Joanne and I, retethered, suck our thumbs and watch our sisters and only brother resume their play among the lifeboats, cables, and deck chairs and delight in watching fish spiral upward from the ocean waves.

Each night we are lulled to sleep by the ship's gentle rocking, ignorant of the fact that our car, purchased by kindly Mennonites and hoisted by a large crane into the dark hold of the ship, nestles quietly beside junk iron for smelting into weapons for Japan. We steam toward India across the vast, lonely oceans in our own miniature world, neither hearing from relatives back home nor gathering news of Hitler's escapades. Yet, the war that will change everything is creeping closer.

CHAPTER 4
Neither Fish nor Fowl

PRESSED UP AGAINST the deck's railing, Dad waves wildly at the lone white man down on the Bombay dock. Missionary Balzer, decked out in a white suit and *topee* (pith helmet) despite the heat, is easy to spot amidst the throngs who are here to view, and exploit if possible, those arriving from that far off land of America. Missionary Balzer's mouth opens and closes like a beached fish, but his shouts are lost in the din. The wharf is teeming with officials who shout orders at dock workers, coolies who loudly claim territory near the gangplank, vendors who scream their wares, and children who clamor for coins tossed from the deck by gullible passengers. Carts creak dangerously near the edge of the dock, pulled by thin, sweat-drenched men ready to receive our luggage as it is disgorged from the bowels of the ship. Horse-drawn, and even man-powered, *jetkas* (rickshaws) line up by the dozen, their owners desperate for our business. Some horses appear too thin to pull even these light carriages; other horses have bags of feed tied around their necks and take advantage of this slack moment to lower their heads and munch. All swish their tails to flick off swarms of hungry insects. Dirty, ill-clad children and mangy dogs dash in and out of it all, ignoring the whacks and curses rained upon them.

We have arrived. In all the hustle, I am unaware that the subtle process of our becoming not quite Indian but no longer American has begun. Somewhat like the snakes that will silently shed their skins over our doorways at night and never be quite the same, now and forever, we will be hybrids.

Missionarying is urgent business, so Mr. Balzer impatiently shouts orders to the coolies who manage to make the task of collecting our baggage appear worth more than the few *rupees* promised them. Our family is distributed among several brightly painted and festooned *jetkas*, our bags tied safely to a cart, and we are off, bound for the train that will carry us inland.

The heat is oppressive, but the sounds, sights, and smells are an assault and serve to speed the process of our transformation. Cows, water buffalos, camels, and even an occasional elephant, slow our progress. Our driver's screams and curses make no impact, nor do the whistles and shouts of the police who stand on podiums in the midst of it all. Cars, buses, bicycles, motorbikes, and animal-powered vehicles of all sorts intermingle in their efforts to move in one direction or another, although which way is not clear.

Everywhere straight-backed women walk purposefully and carry burdens in large, overflowing baskets perched on their heads, faces fairly hidden by the loads. Entire families of beggars line the sidewalks, waiting patiently for alms. Some cuddle against walls streaked red with bettlenut, spat by chewers whose lips also retain the crimson juice. Open stalls offer buyers bright clothing, pots and pans, freshly plucked chickens, and sparkling jewelry, anything that can garner a few coins. Bananas, mangoes, oranges, and foods I have never tasted hang across store fronts, like Christmas decorations. Women squat before small dung-fed fires, cooking the day's meal that sends out wafts of enticing spices that mix with the odors of excrement, dust, fuel, sweat, fresh and rotting vegetables, and meats.

And, oh, the noise! Drivers honk, animals bray, bellow, or cluck, hooves clip clop, and hawkers and shopkeepers scream their wares. It seems everyone and everything has something to say, all undecipherable.

Arriving at the train station, we make our way past weary travelers sleeping on benches and in dirty corners; we carefully avoid stray dogs sniffing for garbage and look away when beggars thrust empty bowls at us. Mr. Balzer hustles us aboard a train that spews steam and covers us in soot before we even board. "First class," Mr. Balzer proudly points out, but Mom frowns at the dirt and reeking toilet in the washroom attached to our compartment. Has she forgotten the travails of her first term here? Have a few short years in America and the birth of a couple of children erased her memory? Doesn't she remember that for us, India is permanent, at least for the next seven years; that this land is now our country to have and to hold? That India is reality, America is the fantasy?

We begin the journey across the hot, dusty, treeless plains, land that stretches out in shades of brown with only an occasional tree or clump of rocks to break the horizon. The train chugs past mud-hutted villages, gaudy temples, wet fields where bent-over women plant rice, and dirt roads lined with oxen-drawn *bundies*. Buffaloes, cooling their bellies in small ponds, turn to stare stupidly at our passing. Everywhere the people's brightly colored clothing stands in stark contrast to the dirt. The women's *saris* and men's *dhotis* in crimson, sapphire, gold, and violet boldly defy these people's poverty.

The train windows offer four choices—glass, wooden shutters, screens, or nothing-at-all. We choose the nothing so as to hang our heads out of the windows and vigorously wave to the children, a human connection with this land. The children wave back, enchanted by either the train or us—or both.

We travel for two days, through Hyderabad City, and beyond. When we run out of cities and even towns, the railroad ends. We transfer to Mr. Balzer's car and bounce across the final miles on washboard dirt roads. As we enter the mission compound, the monkeys, swinging in the trees, scold our passing. The driveway is marked by painted-white stones at the end of which is an enormous, white-washed, two storied bungalow. This, at last, is Kalavakurthy, our home. The road is thronged with men in white *dhotis* and women in brightly colored *saris,* clothing gifted to them upon their baptism. They rush to garland us with strings of marigolds, shower us with gifts of bananas, papaya, and mangoes, and tell us how happy they are that we have come. They enthusiastically embrace us, love us on sight.

We hesitate at this moment of truth. As Ruth once said, "Thy people shall be my people." In like kind, we must go forward, love them in return; there is no going back.

The Mission House

CHAPTER 5
Finding Mama's Lap

HINTS OF HITLER'S intents and talk of war vanish upon our arrival at the Kalavakurthy mission station, which is so isolated that news of the outside world seeps in so slowly and so late that its importance seems of little value, certainly not to our lives. Our arrival here, though, creates a great fuss. The People, as Dad terms the multitudes, have greeted us joyfully, garlanded our necks, and now wait expectantly for increased blessings from God by way of this missionary.

While The People are pleased at our arrival, I am not so happy. Before we are even settled in, my extra mothers, Phyllis and Grace, being the oldest, are shipped off to the hills to get educated, not to return for many months. Betty and Paul are anxious, knowing their turn is coming soon. But Joanne and I are far too little for boarding school, too little to be left unwatched, and far too young to easily learn the rules for living in this strange land, rules ever so different from those in that now far off place from which we came.

So a new set of mothers is quickly hired—our *ayahmas*—who have strict orders to keep Joanne and me safe from snakes, scorpions, mad dogs, and large ants, whose bites leave swollen itchy welts. A thin, gray-haired woman, whose earlobes flop about because they are stretched almost to her shoulders by weighted earrings, is hired to be my *ayah*. She proudly wears the new, gold-bordered, red *sari* wrangled from mother as a condition of the hiring. The *sari* is wrapped tightly around her with the loose end flipped over her shoulder, ready to be retrieved for use as a blanket to shield me from drafts or as a handkerchief to wipe my nose or the dirt from my face. My *ayah* follows me about all day and has a lap that is lovingly available upon demand. She is not at all like Paul's former *Fat Ayah* who sat all day hollering for Paul to stay nearby so she wouldn't have to waddle around chasing after him.

Mornings, our *ayahs* sit cross-legged in the shade of a tree with us in their laps, carefully checking our heads for lice. "Ayee-e-e," my *ayah* shrieks gleefully as she picks an errant louse from my scalp and deftly snaps it between her thumb nails; the small pop tells us it is killed dead, never to bother me again. Mom says, "Head lice are nothing. It's body lice to worry about." When we complain about the head checks, she recounts the story of my grandparents who were missionaries before us. Grandma took pity on and adopted a poor, dirty orphan girl, about twelve years old. The first order of business was to bath the child and rid her of her lice, both head and body. Clean of the vermin for the first time in her life, the frightened child scuttled under the nearest bed, took fever, and died a few days later. "All that poor girl owned was her lice, and Grandma took that away," Mother says as though this will make her point. I think it makes mine.

After the morning head check, my *ayah* surreptitiously pulls out her *beetlenut*—some green leaves over which she smears a thick paste and pops into her mouth. She chews contentedly, although Dad says that God's tobacco and alcohol rule includes *beettlenut* so *ayah* sneakily spits the red juices behind a bush.

Under our *ayahs'* tutelage, Joanne and I quickly learn not to drink the water unless it comes from the *kujahs* lined up like soldiers on a stand on the back verandah, water that has been boiled, cooled, and boiled again. We soon ignore the multitude of smells that numb our nostrils—odors from open drains, urine, sweat, coconut oil, and curries cooking in blue smoke from cow dung fires. These smells all entwine to form what we will eventually learn to know fondly as the wonderful scent of India.

If the black crows perched on the verandah don't caw us awake each morning, the hawkers, barking for a sale of bananas, glass bangles, or some pieces of junk, do. Our *ayahs* hurry in to dress us, coaxing us into shoes despite the heat, and stuff porridge and our daily dose of cod liver oil down our throats. Meanwhile, a servant collects the chamber pots and empties them in a nearby field which will be taxed at a higher rate for these valuable contributions to the crops.

Joanne and I quickly learn to stay close to our *ayahmahs,* but longing for Mama's lap, I slip away and find her on the back veranda in her missionary dress that reaches modestly to her ankles, just meeting her socks and brown tie-shoes. She barters for our food, arguing at length with the throngs of peddlers who rush to surround her—rice, bananas, a little bit of meat, and a liter of buffalo milk. Only enough for today; it will spoil by tomorrow without refrigeration.

"Two *rupees*," a man in a dirty *lungi* holds up a basket of large, red-orange, juicy mangoes. My mouth waters. I tug at Mother's skirt.

"One," she responds, obliging me.

"Oh-o-oh, my family is starving," whines the vendor. "One *rupee,* five *annas,*" he adjusts his price.

"One *rupee,* two *annas,*" and they settle for one *rupee* three *annas.* He smiles, thinking he has bested her; she frowns, knowing he has. For the next hour she bargains her way through the rations for the day. Her lap is hidden somewhere beneath that dress, I know, but I sure don't want to barter for it.

The relationship between an *ayah* and her charge is complicated. While she is the boss, she also isn't. I am a *memsahib,* so I am above her in class. An outcaste, she is from the lowest of the low. When Mom tells her to check my head for lice, *ayah* can demand my obedience. On the other hand, when I trudge off in search of my mother, my *ayah* must follow. Sometimes we find Mama in the back yard, sweat dripping down from under her *topee,* arguing vehemently with the *dhobi.* He has washed our clothes in a nearby pond, first soaking the laundry in lye, then pounding out the dirt on a rock, and finally draping the clothes on the bushes to dry. His heavy black iron, stoked with hot coals, has flattened out each piece, erasing all wrinkles. But

Mom is angry; the buttons on her favorite dress are broken and the zippers rendered useless by the rocks. He is bewildered. Why doesn't she wear *saris* whose eight or ten yards of cotton have no fastenings at all? Her voice rises to an unChristian-like scream. This is not a good time to beg for her lap! I leave.

I quickly learn to love the spicy curries, our staple, which is finger-fed to me by *ayah* when I am too tired or too little to go to the table. Using only the tips of the fingers of her right hand, she carefully works the rice in with the sauce to form a bite-sized ball which, with the push of her thumb, she deftly slips into my mouth. I try to do it myself but drip curry all down the front of me. I must never, never let my left hand—or hers—touch the food; that hand is reserved for bottom washing and wiping, she explains.

As we grow older, Joanne and I are permitted to sit with Mom and Dad around the white-clothed dining room table. British style, the servants arrive with platters of rice, bowls of spicy toppings, chutneys, bananas, and golden mangoes, which they politely offer to each of us in turn. The servants are in cahoots about my need to learn to speak Telegu.

At the table, I demand some rice.

"*Meru Telugu martlardavalenu*" (you must say it in *Telugu*) is David's response as he holds the platter temptingly near my nose. Dressed all in white—turban, *lungi*, and shirt—he waits patiently, scratching one bare foot against the other.

"*Telegu radu*," I pout, indicating that I can't speak the language.

"*Martlardakapote meku bhojanam evanu*," (I won't serve you until you do), he replies. And so goes the war over the filling of my stomach. Baby sister Joanne smiles as Mom carefully chews each bit of meat before placing it in her mouth. I'd rather fight with David now and push Joanne down later when her *ayah* turns her back.

I love the curry but hate the afternoon naps that follow. Joanne and I must lie quietly for at least an hour while a coolie tosses buckets of water on the mats covering the windows to keep us cool.

"I can't sleep," I whisper to Joanne.

"Sh-h-h," she tries to quiet me. "You'll wake her," meaning my *Ayah*, who lies sleeping on the floor beside the bed. "Better not," Joanne says as I creep out to find Mother.

Shoes and dress discarded, the sheet drawn up over Mother's soft body, her rhythmic breathing draws me to her; I want to touch her, smell her. But Dad lies beside her, snoring louder than *ayah*. I'd rather tangle with an angry tiger than risk waking him; my feet make no sound as I pad back to bed.

Ayah teaches me some Telegu words which I practice on the cook's children, who live in a mud hut in the compound. We play, chasing each other, throwing stones at stray dogs, and push around a ball crudely woven from palm fronds. I want so badly to fit in, be one of them, so I ask them to wait while I run inside to put on my own little *sari*. Maybe looking like them will do the trick, disguise my white skin. Alas, when I rush back out, the girls giggle and run away. Dejected, I go in search of Mother for solace and find her sitting in a chair under a banyan tree, encircled by women who sit cross-legged on the ground, listening to her Bible lesson. That Bible in her lap is a clear Do Not Disturb sign.

Late afternoons are no better. Mother is busy dispensing medicines from the back porch cupboard—sulfa for infections, ointments for sores, and pills for malaria. No lap in sight.

Toward evening, the servants light the lanterns and the *ayahs* perform their final chores for the day. Joanne and I whine as they drag us upstairs to dowse us with buckets of water to cleanse our dusty bodies. The sweeper woman who empties the row of tin toilets has fetched the bath water in large buckets and carried them all the way from the tank that holds the water drawn from the well. Two oxen, hitched to a yoke, back up to let a large, buffalo-skin bag down into the cool water, then, as they pull forward, the bag lifts; at the top the bag is tipped into a drain leading to a large cement holding tank—all this to furnish our household with water.

As we are vigorously washed by the *ayahs*, I watch the water rush to the portion of the room that is slanted toward the drain in the corner.

From the drain, the wash water will empty, unwasted, out into the garden. I shudder, remembering that day when a rat darted in through the drain pipe and ran up my leg; my shrieks sent it running back out, more frightened than I.

Before Mother coaxes us into bed and makes certain the mosquito netting is snuggly tucked all around under the mattress, forming a house within a house, and, before she leaves a lantern for safety, before we fall asleep to the sounds that drift over the compound wall—women wailing, babies crying, coolies calling to one another, trains whistling in the distance, and shrill, rhythmic dance music from the cinema that flows far into the night—before all that, Dad insists that the day end with down-on-your-knees Devotions. By lantern light we sing hymns, listen to him read from the Bible, and kneel in prayer. Hunched over our chairs, bottoms pointed toward the sky, every man, woman, and child—and guests if we have any—is expected to pray aloud, Dad's prayer being the longest. I grow sleepy at the droning of his supplications for aid for every single person in the world, especially my sisters and now even my brother so far away in boarding school, and requests for mercy for our sins, which he specifies by child to shame us. With all eyes around me reverently scrunched shut, I seize the opportunity. I creep over to Mother and squeeze myself comfortably into that little space between her lap and the chair over which she is leaning, elbows propped on the seat. I nestle my head against her soft stomach, press my body against hers. Finally, I am content. In this topsy-turvey world of India, an upside-down lap will have to do.

CHAPTER 6
Dread

FEAR BEGINS TO strangle me. Not because Dad says that Hitler is on the rampage—he has taken Czechoslovakia, divided up Poland with Russia, and buddied up with Italy which, in turn, is waging war on its neighbors. Britain, France, Australia, New Zealand, and Canada have finally had enough and now declare war on Hitler and his henchmen. The Battle of Britain that Dad describes is terrifying, but a far larger horror looms on my horizon, creating a fear far larger than Hitler could muster in my little soul. Yet, as it turns out, it is Hitler's very war that will be my salvation.

The root of my dread lies in the fact that my sisters and brother— Phyllis, Grace, and then Paul and Betty as well—disappear and then reappear, seemingly without reason. They arrive by train, stay a few weeks, and then vanish. In my early years, I simply do not understand, but as Joanne and I grow older, the disappearances begin to make sense. It is this understanding, though, that creates the tendrils of fear, a dread that invades my body, seeps into every part of my being, so that, at times, I think I can't breathe.

"Letters, letters from the children," Mom says from time to time. Sensing my question, she adds, "from school, in Kodai. You remember."

"Oh, good!" I need to be reminded again and again that my sisters and brother are alive, not whisked off to the Heaven that awaits us as promised on Sunday mornings. The letters contain descriptions of classrooms, teachers, hikes through the mountains, and many friends; other than complaints about what is served for supper, they even sound cheery. I know, though, that this is the place to which I will be taken and deposited. It will be soon. But when?

I am afraid to ask but know the answer when the *dergi* is sent for to sew new clothes for me but none for my sisters. My body has betrayed me by growing older, larger, ready for the inevitable separation. Even Mother doesn't look happy but puts her usual cheerful spin on the situation.

She says, "You'll look so nice in this yellow when you go to school," and "Would you like ruffles on the bottom of this dress?" and "You'll be prettier than all the other girls!" Does she not notice that I can't tie my shoes or button all the buttons? When she mentions bedding for my bunk at school, I flee. I know I will certainly die if I must climb into a single bed at night, far from home, surrounded by strangers, and, worst of all, without my sister Joanne to cling to. We are practically twins—more than twins, in fact. She cries when I cry and takes my hand in thunder storms. Bravely, she even takes my punishments alongside me. Has nobody noticed that I can't sleep without Joanne beside me?

My turn comes in May, when the scorching heat, muggy air, and soaring temperatures send missionaries scurrying for the hills. Taking advantage of our sisters' and brother's short, mid-term vacation from boarding school, Mom, Dad, Joanne, and I make our way to Kodaikanal and set up housekeeping in a rented forest cottage near the school. We are a whole family again, at least for a few weeks.

The saving of souls left behind, we have grand picnics, hike through the pungent eucalyptus forests, and go boating and punting on the lake below the school. Nobody notices that I sneak away each afternoon to cry, to take a practice run at the pain that will shortly arrive when my parents leave me behind. To my dismay, the ache does not diminish like the release of steam from a train's valves. Instead, the hurting simply increases.

That first day, before my parents leave, Phyllis leads me to my kindergarten classroom like a lamb to the slaughter, her heart as heavy as mine. "It's only for a few months, till you go home. Soon, for Christmas; just think about Christmas," she says and pries my hand loose to hand me over to Auntie Powell, a kindly, gray-haired, kindergarten teacher who greets me as though I were her long lost child. Still, I crouch in my seat, too frightened now even for tears. What if Mom and Dad leave, sneak back to the plains to save souls while I am held captive here in school? When Auntie Powell turns her back, I race upstairs to Phyllis' classroom and roll myself into a ball beneath her seat. Patiently, Phyllis returns me to Auntie Powell, who clucks and sighs and even hugs me, but, as soon as she turns her back, I begin the process all over again.

With bags packed, Dad delays. He paces about muttering about Hitler and the Japanese invading Burma.

"She is too young," Mom nods in my direction. Has she seen my tears, watched my appetite disappear to almost nothing, and noticed my unwillingness to leave her side? Or did the teacher send her a message?

Dad frowns absentmindedly, "Hmm." He turns and looks at me as though he has never seen me before.

I scream, "No, no, don't leave me," but only in my head. Instead, I freeze, unable to plead my case before this mighty man who holds my fate.

In a rare moment of defiance, Mother declares, "She is going along, back to the plains." And just like that, it is decided.

Safely out of reach of the boarding school's tentacles and back at the mission station, what once was a strange land with unusual customs is now a welcomed haven, so comfortingly familiar. I know now that this place is where I want to be; this is my home. Thoughts of boarding school quickly recede, like a bad dream.

Dad complains, "We can't get any news of the war here. I want to know what's going on." Nevertheless, his mutterings about Hitler subside.

Yet, Joanne and I become bored. We have roamed every inch of the mission compound to which we are confined. High walls enclose the five acres or so within which are two bungalows, one for the two missionary ladies who teach and nurse the sick and one two-storied house for our family. Also within the compound are a little, white-washed church, a small hospital, a few sparse rooms for a school, student boarding quarters, and mud huts for the servants. Our *ayahs* have been dismissed as we are now considered to be School Age Children, so the sport of bothering them is not longer a choice.

Dad's missionary zeal rescues us. "Mother, can you find some use for a girl, something for her to do around the house?" Dad asks, bringing forth a shy, frightened, and very dirty girl of about ten.

Mother frowns, "What am I to do with one more? The house is already overflowing with servants." Young, destitute men and women, who are eager to attend school, earn their keep by making our beds, serving our meals, sweeping the floors, and helping the cook. "We don't have any more money. You know the mission board doesn't cover servants' salaries."

Dad says, "Her uncle is here; the mother died yesterday."

"Her father?" Mom asks, still grasping for a way out.

"Doesn't want her." The clincher.

Sugnanama stands on the porch, a tiny stick of a thing with frightened eyes peeking out above the rags she holds tightly in her fist, wadded up and held against her mouth. No sound.

"I guess she can watch the girls," Mother justifies the decision to keep her.

Sugnanama is bathed and deloused, but her rags will be burned later to kill the lice. Indicating that Sugnanama is to follow, Mom, Joanne, and I walk out of the compound and across the road to the bazaar. I normally love the smells of the oil, kerosene, fruit, curries, and dust; the clamor of the crowds and the jingling of the bells that hang on the *jetkas*, a message for the crowds to part, and the whining, nasal, music which sounds ever so worldly to our hymnal-trained ears. But this time my attention is on Sugnanama, who seems more like one of India's wild creatures; nothing like me at all.

The *dergi* steps forward to measure Sugnanama for a *lungi* and blouse, to be sewn and delivered later in the day. She crouches fearfully in the corner. He jerks her roughly forward and takes the measurements, rebuking her for being ungrateful for what the gods have seen in their mercy to grant her miserable soul. No response.

"What color?" Mom points to the stack of brightly colored *saris*. Sugnanama, trained to be invisible, still says nothing, so I pick a bright burgundy with a gold border, my favorite colors. Trudging home, Joanne and I plead for sweets, so Mom stops a passing vendor and mollifies us with *jelabiis* and has some *hulva* wrapped in newspaper for later. The honey from the *jelabiis* drips deliciously down our chins. Sugnanama lowers her rags to nibble and then smiles, ever so slightly. It is with this simple gesture that Sugnanama opens the gate, a first step in the long journey called trust.

Back at the compound, the gatekeeper has allowed the bangle peddler into the compound. What are new clothes without jewelry? Squatting, the woman has her glass bracelets displayed on a cloth spread out on the dirt. The gold, silver, ruby, and indigo colors flash "Buy me!" in the sunlight.

"Mom, please," Joanne and I plead in a whine learned from street beggars. "Just a few *annas*, please." These beautiful bracelets will sparkle on our wrists for a few glorious days before they inevitably break. She relents. The woman kneads our palms, folds them, and then pushes and pulls glass bracelets onto our tiny wrists, the bangles so tight they must be purchased, worn, or broken.

"Even her?" the peddler hides her distain for this small outcaste, although she is one herself.

"Oo-o-oh," I say, admiring the jewels twinkling against Sugnanama's brown skin, so much prettier than against our washed-out white.

She smiles again and lets out a small, "Ah-h-h," twisting her arms back and forth to catch the sun.

"I'm going touring," Dad says at lunch one day, "Mother, you look like you need a rest from the children." She packs our things, tells him to take good care of Joanne and me, and seems almost happy to see us leave.

The car bumps along over washboard roads, slower than usual with the home-made trailer house dragging behind. We stop at night, and Aaron, the cook, starts a small fire beside the trailer to prepare our evening meal. Sugnanama silently arranges her bedding beneath the trailer and ours inside. Dad lights the large lantern, visible for miles around on these flat plains. The glow quickly draws a crowd. Meanwhile, listening to the buzzing of myriad bugs drawn inexorably to the lantern, Joanne and I fall asleep in our bunks. We are comforted by the rise and fall of Dad's voice, alternately promising the rewards of Heaven and threatening fire and brimstone for sins, which he outlines in detail. The next day we are off again to visit another mud-hutted village a few miles, but several hours, away.

On our return, the advent of Sugnanama continues to relieve the boredom and isolation. Wise in the ways of India, and bolder now, at least when out of sight of white missionaries, Sugnanama shows us how to enjoy this land. She entices us to shed our shoes and shuffle our toes in the dust, tip over ant hills that tower as tall as Dad, and taste the wild berries that grow along the edge of the compound wall. She teaches us not to reach for a rock or thrust a hand into a crevice, and shows us how to move safely away from lurking snakes or scorpions. She steers us away from the well for fear we will fall in. We practice carrying brass *kundahs* on our heads without holding on to their sides and even challenge each other to fill the vessels with water, dousing ourselves more often than not.

In turn, Joanne and I teach Sugnanama to play hopscotch, marking patterns in the sand with a stick; mix water with dust to make clay figures; and make paper dolls from the glamorous models in the Sears and Roebuck Catalog. We have become a trio; Sugnanama is no longer The Ghost, and life is good.

Even an unexpected visit from Dad's cousins, Uncle John Wiebe and Auntie Viola, is welcomed, although Sugnanama quickly disappears when David and Paul, the Wiebe twins, emerge from the car, their older brothers and sisters also being away in boarding school. The twins, Joanne, and I quickly wander off, enjoying this expansion of playmates. Aaron is ordered to prepare a special chicken curry and some *dahl* for lunch. So starved are our mothers for female companionship that we children could have screamed, "Cobra!" and they would have likely said, "Hush. Not now." Dad and Uncle John sequester themselves in the office for covert missionary conversation. When they drive off at dusk, small boys chase the car down the drive and even out the gate, the dust only adding another layer to their already dirt-encrusted skin.

The Wiebes are barely out of sight before Dad drops the bomb. "Burma," he says after they leave. "John says that the Japanese are now in Burma, Mother." The worry lines deepen on Mom's forehead when he adds, "The slaughter, torture, you can't imagine, John tells me. First Hitler, now Mussolini . . . I don't know; I just don't know. John thinks we should stay for the duration of the war, not risk those enemy waters. It would take six weeks to reach New York, the way we would have to go, around Africa. Should we stay? Go?"

"What does God want us to do?" Mom says. I glance upward expectantly, but neither God nor emissaries appear.

Over and over again our parents ask each other, "Should we bring the children home from school? Are they safe?"

Alarmed, Joanne and I ask, "Are we going to be captured?" "Will they take Sugnanama too?" Mom and Dad resort to their native

German. *"Vorshicht, die kinder haben ohr"* (be careful, the children have ears). Then they forget about our ears when Pearl Harbor is bombed, the United States and Britain declare war on Japan, and Hitler pompously claims war with the United States.

Dad is now certain, "The Japanese will invade India. We just don't know when." With a meaningful glance at Mother, he adds, "Our daughters."

Meetings with other missionaries ensue, telegrams fly, the children in the hills are sent for. We will return to America; the Wiebes and some others will stay. Ignored, confused, fearful, and without understanding, Joanne and I turn to each other. We devise a game to bring order to the surrounding chaos.

"I'll be Hitler," I declare.

Joanne complies, "I'll be Mussolini. Sugnanama can be the Japanese."

We strut about, join hands, and chase each other madly around and around the compound, pointing and shrieking, "Hitler," "Mussolini," "Japanese." Twirling wildly, we laugh, and laugh, and laugh.

CHAPTER 7
Watermelon for Supper

AS IT TURNS out, Uncle John Wiebe was right. The Japanese did not come to southern India, nor did they assault, murder, or rape any missionary children. The newsmen told of bloody battles at Kohima and Imphal, but were happy to report that, in the end, the Japanese failed to take India. The Wiebe family remained "for the duration," as Uncle John termed it. As you already know, we risked life and limb when we made that dangerous voyage back to the Promised Land of America. The Methodists might say, "That's the roll of the dice;" Dad, knowing dice to be in the sins category, said, "God works in mysterious ways." Either way, we made it safely back to the United States, despite the Germans and the Japanese. All the way to Grandma's house in Minnesota.

"Don't run in the house!" Grandma admonishes from her command-post rocking chair from which nothing escapes her.

"Be quiet," Phyllis, Assistant Mother Number One, rules from the kitchen.

"Stay out of the way," Grace, Assistant Mother Number Two, hisses from the dining room.

What's this? I thought we were safe now at Grandma's house in Minnesota. We've escaped enemy torpedoes, even weathered measles and chickenpox when we sailed all the way from India. Why do we have to tiptoe now? There are no Japanese here. What's going on?

Dad, sipping coffee, takes pity on me and leads me by my hand through the library to the back parlor where the Don'tYouDareSitOnIt velvet sofa has been pushed aside. Mom lies in a bed that shouldn't be there. Seeing her tucked under the covers, I become anxious all over again. She must be dying.

No, she isn't dead because she smiles and points to a white bas-ket beside her, "Your new sister; her name is Margaret Suzanne."

"A baby?" I say, relieved. But a baby? That's what the fuss is all about? I peer at her little wrinkledy face. Well, Dad always says, "God will provide," but He mostly provides us with girls, I see.

The war is still raging on the other side of the world, and we have camped at Grandma's for about six months now. Once again, we are waiting for The Call and, apparently, for Margaret to be born. I don't mind. We have an abundance of cousins here who teach Joanne and me to swim, and they spend hours with my sisters, my brother, and me, exploring the mysteries of Grandpa's enormous garden outside of town. The cousins even provide roller skates so Joanne and I can join their dash up and down the block and around the corner past the library, daring each other to go near the funeral home, although never after dark. First grade is even tolerable here in Minnesota because Grandma now walks me part-way the first few days, the result of throwing myself on the floor and screaming. I feared that this school would swallow me up like the boarding school in India had ingested my older sisters, spitting them out for only a few weeks at Christmas and again in May, during the hot season. Grandma promises that this is absolutely not a boarding school; they don't even want me after three o'clock.

Grandma's house is the entire second floor of Grandpa's half-a-block square Jungas Hardware Store. When my sisters and I get bored, we can lean across the radiators that line the front windows and watch everything that goes on down on Main Street, especially on Saturday nights when all the farmers come to town in their Chevys and Ford pickups. We know who shops where and even what they buy. We listen intently to private conversations; nobody thinks to look up. We watch our cousins, who just might go to Hell because they go to the liberal General Conference Mennonite Church instead of our Mennonite Brethren Church. They are actually allowed to go to the popcorn-smelling movie show two doors down, well in sight of our perch. I do so envy these cousins, even if movies are sinful here in America. Sometimes I am just plain weary of being different.

Then, just like that, our briefly normal American life is disrupted when Dad announces that the long awaited Call has finally come. It didn't come at the dinner table or when we were gathered for evening prayers; not even by telegraph or long distance. No burning bush. No tablets of stone. Just a secret command to Dad to make a trip across the desert and over the mountains to California.

But we have no furniture, no car, and certainly no money. At first Mother fusses about leaving Grandma once again, this time all the way across the country, two weeks' drive at least, which is actually nothing compared to halfway around the world like India. But Dad doesn't remind her of that.

"I have so little time with them. Besides, what if my parents get sick? How will I get back?" she complains, wringing her hands. She turns to the practical aspects of this Call, "What about furniture? Dishes? Bedding?" She tries her best, but you just can't argue with God and Dad's determination.

"God will provide," Dad is always so very certain. As proof, God sends us a small car by way of the Minnesota church folks, and we are on our way. Phyllis, Grace, Betty, Joanne and I ride in the back seat; Mom, Dad, and Paul in the front; and baby Margaret gets the best seat in the house, a sling hung between the front and back seats, window to window. I am given wide berth because of my car sickness. All I have to do to maintain my window seat is to moan now and then, jump out when everyone yells, wait for Dad to hastily jerk to a stop, and vomit. Such a small price to pay to avoid being squished between two sisters.

It takes weeks to make the trip, although some days we log one hundred miles and whoop with joy at this accomplishment. We stop for lunch and a nap at city parks, sleep in cheap hotels if necessary, crunch dry cereal unless there is milk for breakfast, gobble bologna sandwiches at noon, and heat canned soup for supper. Margaret's diapers are washed in the sink each evening, and we take turns holding them out the car window by day to dry, just so she can wet them again. We visit cousins in Montana, stop at Mennonite churches to share our missionary experiences to audiences eager for reassurance that their money has gone to save suffering souls and earned them a step closer to Heaven. After the services, we are divided up and sent to sleep at the homes of any members willing to take in a few girls or a boy.

Finally, nearing California, we closely watch the precipices on the hairpin curves as we climb the mountains, the last barrier between us and the small corner of the Promised Land of America that is to be ours. Dad adds to the excitement by shifting to neutral to coast down the steep grades, causing us to scream in delight, the closest thing to a roller coaster that we will ever get. Dad also keeps one eye on the gauges.

"What if the engine overheats?" Mom adds a new worry but already knows Dad's response, "God will provide." As will the extra can of water in the trunk, I think.

We enter the San Joaquin Valley with relief, the engine still on good behavior. Almost there. So Mom returns to her worry about what we will do for furniture, food, money even.

"God will provide," Dad repeats, reaching over to pat Mom's knee. We turn our shared and now growing anxiety into speculation about what God, by way of the California Mennonites, will have prepared for us. How many bedrooms will the house have? Will there be enough beds for so many of us? Will anything be new—of course not. Will the people like us? We lean out the windows, eyeing every detail of our about-to-be new habitat. Suddenly, Paul spots a bright, red and green striped, hand-painted sign, "Watermelons. Cheap."

"Can we, please, please," my sisters and I beg from the back seat. To our surprise, Dad stops.

"Watermelons! Watermelons!" Joanne and I bounce up and down.

This time Dad provides. He shells out twenty-five cents of the remaining few dollars that he borrowed from Uncle John for the trip, and we happily make room on our laps to hold these green-stripedy, juicy globes for the last few miles into town. Following instructions, we make our way to the Mennonite Brethren Church of Reedley, California, in whose hands our family's fate now rests. The minister comes out to greet us warmly, the first good sign, and points to a little yellow house.

"That is the home we have for you, over there on the corner; it's unlocked. I'll stop by tomorrow; I know you're tired. By the way, Mr. Epp is bringing you a rocking chair in the morning." Mom is pleased; she will be able to rock the baby! This is another good sign, and our hopes soar.

Stiffly, we untangle ourselves from each other and the car and hesitantly make our way up the walk to our new home; we are hopeful but still a bit uncertain about what God has in mind here. We walk through the house. The first bedroom is empty. The other sports a double bed, for Mom and Dad, of course; the living room is also devoid of furniture, as is the kitchen. An old ice box that requires daily tending by the ice delivery man is on the back porch. Except for all the neighbors who live closer to us than anyone before, that's it; a bed and an ice box. We check the small rooms again. Nope, no furniture. No chairs, no table, no sofa, no lamps, no dishes, no *dakshas* (cooking utensils), no silverware. We silently gravitate to the living room. Mother's lips are pressed together, disappearing into a thin line, her eyes cold and narrow. For once, Dad has nothing to say. Our combined silence, so heavy our shoulders droop, is suddenly broken by the baby's shrill cry.

"She's hungry," Mother's lips reappear.

Joanne and I sigh and dare to whisper, "Me too."

Mother stands very, very still, gives us a long look, as though she has never seen us before. Then a miracle happens. The twinkle returns to her eyes, and I know that somehow everything is going to be all right.

"What will we eat for supper?" we whine, ever so bold now. We have only the plates, cups, and silverware that reside in our picnic basket, the one pan for warming soup, and no food. But Mother can handle anything.

She laughs and says, "We'll initiate this new house. We'll have one of those watermelons for supper." She bustles about, unpacking the knife that cut all those bologna sandwiches along the way. Her laughter is contagious. "This is going to be another one of those extraordinary occasions that just our family gets to have," she says, and we all agree. Being different sometimes just makes us special.

Joanne and I promptly lead the parade, tromping out to the back yard chanting, "Watermelon, watermelon for supper."

Avoiding Mom's eye, Dad insists that we pray before we eat because that is what we Mennonites do, no matter what. "Thank you, God, for providing us a safe trip and a roof over our heads for the night," then tacks on, "and for our supper." He pauses.

Joanne and I seize the opportunity. "Amen!" we interrupt and then yell, "Let the party begin!"

CHAPTER 8
Don't Tell

THE TOO SMALL, yellow, California house in town is soon discarded in favor of a country home, compliments of Mr. Kunkle, who will exchange the rent for passage into Heaven.

Mom says, "Nobody has to know our business out here," meaning that gossips won't note that we sleep until ten on Saturday mornings, or exclaim over the tattered state of our laundry hung on the lines. Consequently, her favorite admonishment, "What will people think?" falls less frequently from her lips.

Best of all, I come home to Mom and my baby sister every single day. The house is filled with homey smells of baked *zwiebach* and *borscht* and the crisp scent of starched, dampened clothing, ready for ironing. A bus arrives each morning to fetch Joanne, Betty, Paul, and me for our day at Windsor Grammar School, which is one step above a one-room country schoolhouse, having two grades per classroom. Meanwhile, Phyllis and Grace accompany Dad to the Mennonite high school in town. His current Call is to build this four-room high school into something magnificent and to preach sermons at the Mennonite church on Sunday mornings. Mom can't drive, so she is always, always home. Nobody here even mentions boarding school, so this is as close to Heaven as I have ever been. This place is truly The Promised Land of America, the country my sisters so often talked about when we were in India. God is on my side now, I am certain, even if I fib now and then or even tell a really gostraighttohell lie, like I have to just one time.

It is like this. When the California weather is so warm and inviting, riding the stifling bus home after a sweaty day in school is like sitting in the heat of the Indian plains in May. With much persuasion,

Mom has reluctantly agreed that we can occasionally walk home rather than ride that stuffy bus.

On one particularly warm day, Betty says, "Let's walk. Mom won't mind."

"Yes, oh, yes," Joanne and I require no persuasion. We quickly plan to take the longest possible route home in order to extend this moment of freedom from being children of missionaries, offspring who must always behave lest our parents appear less Godly. "Let's see if Marion and Roxy want to go too," we quickly add, extending our invitation to our good friends.

The five of us set off, stopping along the way to sail paper boats in the small rivulets of water that feed the thirsty grape vines paralleling the road. The water originates, though, from wide, river-like, DoNotEverSwimInThemYou'llDrown irrigation ditches that line the highways.

"Don't even think about putting your big toe in those ditches; you'll drown." Mom's command to Joanne and me is as real as if she were right here beside us. Her paranoia even extends to, "No, you can't go along," when my older sisters offer to teach me to swim in a neighbors' dammed up irrigation ditch.

This day is hot, so we dawdle, peering into the murky water of a very large irrigation ditch, at least ten feet deep but ever so inviting. Sailing paper boats just isn't enough. Before we know it, Roxy leaps in, hollering with joy and splashing us with water so cool that the temptation becomes too great.

"Ooo-o- o, you shouldn't," I admonish Roxy but venture forth anyway, removing my shoes and socks. "Don't you dare tell," I command Betty and Joanne. "I'll just wade." My toes sink delightfully into the mud.

Betty, the good sister, says, "Remember what Mom said?" and begins to sing one of Dad's favorite hymns, "Yield not to temptation, for yielding is sin."

With the wages of sin hanging over their heads, Joanne, Marion, and Betty hang back.

"Come on; it's really cold and squishy," I drown out Betty's singing and splash until their shoes are so wet they have no choice but to take them off. With that, temptation wins. Tucking our skirts up into our underwear, the way we used to in India when the car got stuck in a stream, we wade out even farther. We bend over and blissfully immerse our arms all the way up to our elbows.

"Just to wash the dust off," Betty rationalizes.

"Isn't this wonderful? It's freezing!" I wiggle with pleasure, take a step forward, and step on a broken shard of glass. The muddy water mixes with my blood. Mother and God seem to be looking over my shoulder, intensifying the pain that has so quickly replaced my joy.

"Ooooh," gasps Marion.

"Needs stitches," reassuring words from Roxy, the Expert on Disasters. He proudly displays sixteen stitches from an old wound on his leg and four on his scalp.

But Betty, Joanne, and I are of one mind. "Only one thing we can do. We have to hide it, not tell Mom," Betty is certain. Joanne and I agree, no need to confer on this!

My shoe squishes with blood on the long limp home. We dash furtively to the bathroom to wash out the gash, and then soak away the blood from my shoe and sock. We tie the wound with rags, extra thick later for the night, and make ourselves as invisible as possible.

Over the next few days, the process becomes routine—suppress the limp, commandeer the bathroom upon arrival home from school, wash the blood-stained sock, hang it to dry out of sight on the back side of my bed, tie up the foot with clean rags for the night, bury last night's soaked rags in the grape fields, and look angelic at breakfast. As long as we don't quarrel, we are generally ignored anyway.

Miraculously, we get by with it. The wound heals, and no suspicion has been cast our way, no ensuing punishment. We are masters of deceit and rather proud of it.

Many years later, I will sit at my own table with my visiting mother at the head, my husband at the foot, happily surrounded by my own sweet children. As usual, my mother regales my darlings with stories of her travels and adventures, of which she has an endless supply. Finally, the tales include those of my growing up years.

One child interrupts eagerly, "Did you know about Mom cutting her foot in the irrigation ditch?"

My mother doesn't. So the children enthusiastically share the telling of the story, talking all at once, an unexpected and rare opportunity to turn the tables, get me into trouble for a change. I, who would lay down my life for them! Right before my eyes, they are transformed into imps. They embellish the depth of the water, the size of the wound, and the degree of my intrigue and deception. They finish with a flourish and wait with bated breath, eyes intent upon their grandmother. A long silence ensues.

"What?" my Mother is finally aware that she is expected to respond.

"Well?" these angels-turned-devil ask in unison, edging forward in their seats, moving in for the kill, their chance to see my blood flow, just as it did that day in the forbidden irrigation ditch.

My mother knits her brow, still baffled.

In one voice they cry, "Aren't you going to punish her?" unbelief written all over their faces.

Mother laughs, "Oh, no. It's too late now."

The children's shoulders sag with disappointment, but mine don't. While few of my sins escape God and Mother's wrath, this one does, not only once but twice!

CHAPTER 9
Grapes and Paper Dolls

DAD CLAIMS THE grape fields that surround our house are a blessing from God. My sister Joanne and I think picking grapes in the hot sun in dusty California in the summer of 1943 is about the worst possible intrusion into our precious escapefromschool time. We wonder if God knew what he was doing when he invented them. Yet in the end, these grape fields do yield one of our greatest pleasures—paper dolls.

At the close of each school year, most other children look forward to a long lazy summer, lying about doing whatever rich kids do. I have no clue what that is. But our family is poor, and we must do whatever we can to add to Dad's meager salary in order to buy what Mom says we need. I don't know for sure, but I guess that means food because whatever is placed on the table, mostly macaroni and cheese, disappears as soon as Dad says, "Amen." So there are the grape fields all around us, ready and waiting for our family of nine to endure the heat and drip buckets of sweat so others can enjoy raisins in their breakfast cereal.

Thus, when school is out, Dad says, "We'll start early tomorrow. Gwen and Joanne, you too."

"Do we gotta?" Joanne and I cry.

"I'm only seven; she's six," I say, pointing to Joanne. "We're too little."

"Stop whining," snaps Older Sister Grace. Easy for her to say. It's her turn to stay home, tend baby Margaret, wash clothes, clean the house, make sandwiches for our lunch break, and cook supper. Piece of cake compared to facing a long day in the dust.

"We're sick," we try again. Dad gives us his Look. Subdued and dejected, we quietly drag out our most raggedy old clothes, move our breakfast cereal as slowly as possible from the bowls to our mouths, then finally take up our curved knives, a mason jar of ice water, and join the rest. Like a row of elephants, from largest to smallest, we trail out to the fields, no jolly "Heigh ho, heigh ho, it's off to work we go," from us.

Joanne and I choose a row closest to the house but far from the rest of the family. Thus, we can lounge about without a "Get back to work" or "What do you think you're doing?" The row is so long that when we look down it the cars on the road at the end look small. We peer at the vines, so heavy with leaves that they hide the large bunches of green grapes that droop within them. Miniature dried-up irrigation troughs run parallel to the grape vines.

Discouraged already, we whine some more, but this time Dad, who is helping us get started, takes unexpected pity on us and offers an incentive. "When you fill one hundred trays, you can quit for the day," he says.

At a penny a tray, that is a whole dollar. Though the dollar won't see the insides of our pockets, we brighten at the prospect of finishing early, maybe even by lunch, if we really work hard. Optimistically, we grab a wooden frame, about eighteen inches wide and two and a half feet long, and a handful of brown paper sheets. We carefully lay a sheet of paper on the ground, perpendicular to the rows of vines, and fix the frame so that it borders the paper. We scoot under the vines and search for bunches of juicy, green grapes, hanging so camouflaged under the matching leaves that the task becomes a game of Hide and Seek. Each find is followed by a swift cut of the knife at the top of the bunch with one hand and a quick catch with the other. The final step is to crawl out from under the arbor and place the grapes carefully on the brown paper tray. Like yo-yos, we move back and forth between the vines and the paper.

Joanne shrieks, "A black widow," knocking me over in her haste to withdraw from the entangling vines. "You go in," she says and then laughs, "Just kidding."

Our older sisters find joy in terrifying us with stories of these monster spiders. They say, "Black widows will kill you, horribly. Your blood will drip from every pore, your eyes will bulge out, and you'll die so quickly you won't have time to confess your sins. You'll go straight to Hell," and then they make the most of the opportunity by adding, "So you'd better behave, all the time." So we are vigilant, at least when it comes to Black Widow spiders.

Slowly we fill one brown tray and then another, each time spreading the grapes correctly to the edge of the paper but not past the wooden frame. Thus, in a few weeks, when the grapes have turned golden in the hot sun, strong Hispanic men will come in, cover each tray with a clean sheet of paper, and, in one swift motion, flip the tray so that the undersides of the grapes are exposed, ready to brown as well. Phyllis and Grace tried turning trays once, but they hobbled about in such pain for days after that that the episode became a family legend.

From time to time, Joanne and I stop to drink the now warmed water, snack on grapes, and take a short rest. We hear the murmurs of our sisters in a nearby row, but mostly we are left to ourselves. To pass the time more quickly, we speculate about what we would do with the day's dollar were it to come to us instead of the family coffers.

"I want books, maybe even piano music," Joanne says.

"Not me," I say, "I want ice cream, all I can eat!"

We pause, thoughtful for a moment, and then cry in unison, "Paper dolls; we'd get paper dolls!" What we want more than anything else in the world is store-bought paper dolls, not flimsy, home-made papers dolls cut from the Sears and Roebuck Catalog.

Other than store-bought paper dolls, we cherish those created for us by Phyllis and Grace. Dad ruled that any of us can draw and paint paper dolls on Sunday afternoons, God's NobodyCanWork day. Once the painted dolls are dry, they are pasted to cloth for support and then cut out. Any number of clothes can be constructed for such a doll. First the designer traces around the body and then creates dresses, pajamas, and even grand evening gowns for the doll. When painted, the clothes are set aside to dry. Given the hours of work this task requires, it is not easy to wheedle a doll and her wardrobe from either sister, especially Grace. Yet, deep down in our hearts, Joanne and I want more than anything to have some real paper dolls, store-bought. But we are resigned to the knowledge that these are for the rich people like our Minnesota cousins, and we aren't rich, for sure.

By late afternoon Joanne and I have picked enough grapes to fill one hundred trays. Sweat runs down our faces, under our arms, even on our tummies, mixing with the dirt to form streaks of mud.

"You look like a ghost," Joanne laughs at the contrast between the whites of my eyes and my now browned skin.

"So do you," I grin. "Isn't it weird? We're brown now, but everyone else is white. In India we were white and everyone else was brown."

We proudly view the trays of grapes all lined up between the rows of vines, looking ever so much like a ribbon of green piano keys. We have contributed to the family income, helped put food on the table!

At the end of grape-picking season, when our skin seems permanently chocolate-colored from our daily one hundred, hand-picked trays of grapes, Dad gets The Check, payment for our family's labors. He doesn't show it to us, doesn't tell us how much we have earned, but he does do something that takes us by surprise.

"Girls," meaning Joanne and me, "Mom and I are going to town this afternoon to put this check in the bank. You can go along. I'll give each of you a quarter for working so hard; you can spend it anyway you like."

Twenty-five cents? This is a windfall. I've never had twenty-five cents all at one time. This quarter can buy a whole lot of ice cream, but for Joanne and me, there is only one decision to make. What kind of paper dolls will we buy?

Left on our own at the Five and Dime Store, we thumb through the paper doll books temptingly displayed on a rack. One has a family with three children with clothes for each, even pajamas. Another has movie stars such as Rita Hayworth and Hedy Lamarr, whose gowns are so lovely they must be sinful. We long for them, anyway. But the book that Joanne and I absolutely must possess contains a bride, groom, three bridesmaids, three groomsmen, and even a cherub-like flower girl. There are pages and pages of gowns, tuxedos, bouquets of flowers, a three-tiered cake, all which is required for a grand wedding. The clincher is the bride's pure-white piece of loveliness, and it has a train that could trail half the length of a church aisle. Together with the family book, we have it all, the wedding and the guests. We exchange our quarters for the books, and Dad surprises us again by springing for ice cream cones. I sigh; this is about as good as life can get.

Back home, when the dolls are cut out, divided up, and arranged across our bedroom floor, I say, "Joanne, you be the groom; I'll be the bride."

Joanne objects, "Why do I have to always play the groom?" a refrain I will hear many times before those beautiful paper dolls wear out.

I shrug and start singing, "Here Comes the Bride," marching the couple down a make-shift aisle. We become engrossed in our exquisite dolls and entertain visions of falling madly in love with our own princes and talk of our own weddings that will inevitably follow. So, with the toil in the fields behind us and the beautiful dolls before us, it completely slips our minds to kneel in prayer to offer thanks to God for creating grapes.

CHAPTER 10
The Con

"WHAT WILL PEOPLE think?" Mother says to about everything her children do or think about doing. In response, I hastily check my clothing, straighten up my behavior, and look anxiously about. Another favorite is, "Your quarreling will be the death of me yet," the back of her hand on her forehead, eyes turned Heavenward. She mostly means us, GwenandJoanne—one word. We come in pairs in this family, PhyllisandGrace, one word; PaulandBetty, another word; and Margaret, not yet a pair. She might say, "Bring in the wash, GwenandJoanne." Or Dad might say, "PaulandBetty, come help me load the car."

Joanne and I elbow, argue, and scream, sometimes so angry words elude us. "Your gum is in my hair," I complained after a night in our shared bed. "You're hiding my shoes," Joanne accused. "Am not," "Are so," and on it goes.

These quarrels, though, are part of the glue that forms the bond between two sisters who are one year, two months, and a day apart. We hate, and we love, because we desperately need each other, our souls starving for attention in this over-sized family.

Joanne and I find all sorts of advantages to being two in one, much like the two-legged sack races that require concentrated co-operation to cross the finish line. We find that an hour or so a day of piano practice is easier if we play duets, picking one hundred trays of grapes a day is possible when two apply themselves, refraining from the truth and stealing extra war rations of sugar can be ratio-nalized when urged on by the other. When Paul enjoys frightening us by listening to *"Inner Sanctum"* or *"The Shadow"* on the radio, we have each other to cling to. We can surreptitiously play games together during the boring on-your-knees evening prayers, and we always have someone to jump rope with or challenge to a game of jacks. Jacks is important.

"Just once," I say, "I want to beat them. They don't have any chores like we do; they can play jacks all they want, practice all night if they want to." Those Japanese girls who live in the camps and get picked up by our school bus every morning are my enemies, hated because they always win at jacks. For me, the major World War II battle is reduced to the toss of a few spiked pieces of metal and a small rubber ball.

"Want to live in that camp?" asks Betty, referring to the compound where these Japanese Americans now live, a place where men and women silently turn their backs when our school bus gathers up their children. This make-shift camp has long sheds with flimsy walls to mark off cramped living quarters for each family, and hard-packed dirt is all there is for a playground. A tall, barbed wire fence surrounds the camp, creating a barrier that shouts of a gulf wider than the Atlantic Ocean. No matter how hard I stare, I just don't understand.

"No, I don't want to live in that camp, but I hate them; they always win."

"Laugh too, when they win," says Joanne, bringing out the jacks. "Come on; let's practice so we can beat 'em."

While jacks is the challenge at school, ducking chores is the contest at home; one which Joanne and I are also determined to win. A family our size requires considerable maintenance—cooking, cleaning, hanging all those washed and wringer-squeezed clothes out to dry, bringing those clothes back in for ironing, and the three-times-a-day washing mounds of dishes. I hate it all.

Like Cinderella's wicked sisters, mine keep watch. "Get busy," says Grace. "Come on," Betty says. "Says in the Bible you have to," Paul adds his bit. "Where?" I demand, but he just pulls out his whittling knife and begins to whistle as he carves. Mom hums, "Work for the Night is Coming," my least but her most favorite hymn.

When it comes to washing, drying, and putting away nine plates, nine forks, knives, spoons, nine drinking glasses, an assortment of cooking utensils, and even dishes left over from lunch, Joanne and I balk. That's just too many dishes.

So Joanne and I set aside our grievances and scheme. Inspired by the army's heroic victories we learn about from the radio, we cleverly plot our course.

"If there is life on other planets, did God send another Son there to die for their sins as well?" I ask, ever so innocently, at the dinner table. This ploy turns the conversation to our advantage and is good for at least a 30-minute heated debate on planetary life and the scriptures. Or I say, "Paul, tell us that lie again, about how radios are going to some-day have boxes to show us pictures so we can SEE the radio shows." Good for another round of finger-pointing and supposition.

"Let's go," I poke Joanne at such moments, our golden opportunity to slip from our seats, move silently to the bedroom, climb out the window, head straight for the grape fields, run down the row past the outhouse, the wash house, the barn, turn left into the peach orchard, climb a tree, and wait for the piles of dishes to be wiped clean—by somebody else.

Now, the oldest of all of us, Assistant Mother Number One, Phyllis, is sly. The army certainly would parachute her down into enemy territory and win the war if they knew how cunningly she can carry out her mission. She is so clever that, single-handedly, she manages to outwit the combined efforts of us, GwenandJoanne—one word.

It starts during dinner one evening when she calmly says, "I'll tell you a story if you'll dry the dishes tonight, GwenandJoanne." With an offhanded, take-it-or-leave-it smile, she adds with a shrug, "If you like." Now, had it been her more usual, "GwenandJoanne, take a bath now!" or "I'm washing your hair, no argument!" or her latest rule about our crowded dinner table, "It's fair to smear jam on the table to keep your neighbor's elbows out of your space," we would have balked. Instead, she just hooked us like fish begging for bait.

Entertainment, other than hymn singing, is sparse in Mennonite households, so story telling is something we relish, even beg for. And

Phyllis's stories are as good as the chocolate we get on Easter Sunday.

"Okay," I say.

"Just this once," Joanne whispers to me, "not tomorrow night." I nod.

Phyllis begins with those time-honored, magical, spell-binding words, "Once upon a time . . . ." Our fingers flip the dish towels onto automatic while our minds fly with the tale, which is really, really good and will be savored over and over again in the days, even years, to come. Only one problem, the story runs out before the dishes do, the *dakshas* (pots and pans) yet to go.

Another ever so sweetly and innocent-looking smile from Phyllis. "Shall I start another one?" We swallow the bait.

"Yes, Yes," we actually beg for more.

So again, "Once upon a time . . ." and in a flash, the dishes are done, but it's the story that isn't this time.

"Finish it, finish it," we beg. Surely she'll hang around to tell us the ending.

"Sorry, I've got homework to do." She adds, uncertainly, "Maybe tomorrow night." Anything for the finish. "Okay," we agree. Drying dishes just one more time is a small price to pay.

And thus the hook is well set, and she is smoothly reeling us in. Each night a story ends, but a new one begins and, alas, is left unfinished. The bedroom window is open but unused, the grape fields wait but are forgotten, the peach tree branches are left empty.

Phyllis has executed a campaign with military precision, conducted a major *coupe d'etat*, all without lifting a finger or even uttering a harsh word. Like fish netted and flopping helplessly in the bottom of a boat, we have been caught, all without bloodshed or even a single protest, a cry, or a whimper. Thus, totally unaware, the award for superiority in deviousness and cunning slips quietly from the fingers of two young girls to hers.

It takes some time before Joanne and I realize that Phyllis taught us one of life's set-in-stone lessons, "There is more than one way to skin a cat," or "You can catch more flies with honey than vinegar." What we don't know is that the stories and lessons learned from Phyllis are going to be nostalgically relived and appreciated many times over in the years to come, when we return to India, without her.

CHAPTER 11

The Call, Again

LIFE IS PRETTY good here in California. The President of the United States gets on the radio and tells us that the war is finally over and so are the battles over who took more than their share of rationed sugar. Dad even talks about getting good tires for a change. Saving souls in India has withered to memories retold for guests and retold by Dad from the pulpit.

"Amen," we chime in after Paul says the blessing at the dinner table one evening. Following the Amen is the usual, "You're taking too much," "Your elbows are on the table, I can't eat," "Mom, make her stop," "I washed dishes yesterday; I don't have to tonight," "You did not," and "Yes, I did." On this particular evening, Dad is late, not unusual on the days when he drives to Los Angeles and back for his classes at the University of Southern California to get his Master of History degree.

"Mom, is Dad going to take that job?" Grace asks.

"I don't know," Mom says uncertainly, "they really want him."

"Wouldn't it be great to live in Los Angeles? Near a good college?" Betty, who makes straight As, remarks.

"We'd be rich," I say hopefully, envisioning a stop for ice cream every single day after school like my rich cousins in Minnesota do. I think, but don't say out loud, that when Dad teaches at the university, I will be saved from boarding school—forever and ever, Amen.

"Any Mennonites there?" asks Paul. Nobody knows.

Dad's arrival on this day, though, is different. He bursts into the house without a "Hello," or "Why didn't you wait for me?" or "It's sure good to be home," or "Wow, was that a long drive; the traffic was horrible." We look up expectantly. He is smiling, seeming ever so pleased with himself, so it has to be that he has said, "Yes, I'd be honored to join the faculty at your high and mighty school. How soon can I start?"

Instead, he says, "God has Called us back to India."

I drop my fork. No warning, no bugle call, not a whisper from God to ask my opinion, nothing. I don't think I can breathe; my chest hurts; I freeze. Back to India and boarding school? Away from Mom being home every single day, cooking, cleaning, and sewing? Overwhelmed, actually, with so many children, a too small house, and too little time to even pay her children much attention, but home nevertheless. This life is plenty good enough for me. Now, in the twinkling of an eye, our lives are going to be turned completely upside down, again.

"Goodbye," I must say to my best friend, Marion. "Goodbye," I must say to my teachers. "Goodbye, goodbye, goodbye." Why? Why do we have to leave? Always say, "Goodbye?" Always start over again?

"I won't be going. Phyllis either," Grace is defiant, even angry.

Phyllis explains unnecessarily, "College, we're going to college next year."

Leave them behind? We can't go without them; we can't do that. The room turns cold and silent. Nobody looks at Dad. I shiver, then dash from the table, rush out the door, and run far into the grape fields. There, under the arbors, I huddle, curled into a ball, and rock back and forth until Joanne comes looking for me.

When Dad says, "We must go; God has Called us," we must do so immediately, although I don't think that "immediately" was actually in that Call; Dad probably added that part. The first step is to go to Grandma's in Minnesota for The Preparation Period. So we go.

The Minnesota church ladies quickly take charge and direct their zeal to what the church bulletin terms, "Preparing the Hiebert family for India." Every afternoon these kind-hearted ladies bring pins, needles, thread, and the latest gossip to Grandma's house to magically fashion dresses, skirts, blouses, and sturdy under things, enough to provide us for the next seven years because that's how long you stay there at one time. Seven years of clothing for one boy and four girls demands a lot of sewing, but Mennonite women are purposeful. They energetically measure and then estimate what my size will be each year until I finish high school. Being almost eleven, I can't imagine being twelve, much less sixteen or seventeen.

Mother says, "They just don't have good cloth in India; the quality just isn't good." She asks the ladies for extra yardage, "Just in case." Not only is this given, but the church folks collect bedding, linens, dishes, and silverware to be packed in large, metal barrels. When it comes to buying seven years of shoes, the bewildered clerk runs for the boss and probably quit that same day.

The completed clothing is stored in the front parlor, ready for packing into khaki, army surplus footlockers. On top of mine he paints, "Gwendolyn Hiebert, Kodaikanal School, Kodaikanal, South India," so it will go to the right place. This trunk will contain all the clothes and bedding I will need. And all of it is new, unworn, and unfamiliar.

"My doll," I plead with Mom, holding up my most precious and only true possession left to me, all other attachments having been discarded as unfit, even the paper dolls. "Is there room for my last doll, Peggy? Please?" I handpicked this doll from the *Sears and Roebuck Catalogue* at Christmas.

"Your last doll," Mom had said. The choice was easy; this doll was the most beautiful, almost heavenly, of those displayed in the catalogue. She has short, soft, brown hair, and brown eye lashes that close over fat cheeks. She now listens to my secrets and sleeps beside me at night.

I stomp my foot. "I won't go without my doll! You can't make me."

"Not now," Mom says, so preoccupied she is probably traveling the oceans and saving souls in India. Has she already forgotten me?

While the church ladies sew, I help my sisters fix afternoon *faspa*, a tidbit of a meal to reward the women for their service. As we scurry back and forth from kitchen to dining room with coffee and German pastries, Mrs. Thiessen stops me.

"I need you to try on this skirt, see if it fits," she says. The red, plaid skirt has deep pleats all the way around. When she has pinned it to her satisfaction, she says, "I put an extra big hem in the skirt; that way you can lengthen it when you grow taller." I can't help but twirl around and squeal in delight as the skirt billows out like a fully opened umbrella. I'll be able to wear this for years! I come to a quick stop; such enjoyment might be viewed as sinful in the eyes of these Godly ladies, but Mrs. Thiessen smiles and shows me the fabric for the matching jacket she intends to sew. The blouse, already finished, has pearl buttons down the front with lace climbing up and down beside them and even around the collar. I finger the lace, run my hand down the gathered sleeves, and smile.

Minding my Mother's admonishment to always be grateful, I murmur, "Thank you," to Mrs. Thiessen and rush to the kitchen to tell Joanne. "No more hand-me-downs when we get there," I promise her. We are tired of our cousins' cast-offs. While we may dread boarding school, we both long for the day when we will be allowed to wear all these lovely clothes, clothes that we can only touch and not yet wear. They belong to a time to come.

The smells of baked *zwiebach*, fried *roll kuchen*, hot coffee, and steaming dish water waft through the house. My three hundred pound grandma sits lookout in her rocker in the corner of the dining room. From this perch she can monitor the library and parlor to her left and the front sitting room to her right.

From time to time she mutters, "Deserting me," expressing her displeasure at her only daughter's willingness to follow That Man to the mission field. Yet she remains hopeful. She confides in my older sisters that the story of Abraham's willingness to sacrifice Isaac has lifted her spirits. "God intervened at the last minute, saved Abraham from losing his child. So I'm waiting for the intervention," she says. One does not argue with this grandmother.

Meanwhile, since Grandma can't exert her influence on her headstrong daughter, she can do so on the church ladies. She gives orders for packing, inspects the sewing, and shouts orders at us, her granddaughters, as we rush by, constantly setting the table or cleaning up. Sitting around the large dining room table, the ladies compliment Grandma on her jelly, ask for her recipe, argue about how to make the best coffee, comment endlessly on the weather, and exchange the latest gossip about the sick and the needy and the not so needy. Then they tell Mama what nice girls we are. They switch back and forth between German and English, depending on the intensity of the topic.

Late each afternoon, when the ladies leave and the house is quiet and nobody notices, I forget about the lovely dresses and slip into the bedroom that I share with my sisters. I crawl behind the roll-away bed, folded up during the day to make room, and curl up in a little space where nobody will see me. Hidden, I cry quietly over the homesickness that is certain to come when I am in boarding school, a long, long way from home, far from Mom and Dad. I think that if I squeeze out all the loneliness and misery now, maybe it won't hurt as much when that awful day comes, that day when Mom and Dad will kiss us, say goodbye, and we will board the train and wave until long after they are out of sight.

CHAPTER 12

The Day Mama Lost It

NOW WE ARE ready to leave Minnesota for our seven-year sojourn. Dad's passion for traveling has taken our family across many borders. We have gone back and forth between Grandma's home in Minnesota and California on the west coast; we have sailed to and from India, with stopovers in such exotic places as China, Singapore, England, and Europe. We have packed in as many states and countries as possible. God doesn't mind if we take circuitous routes to our destinations as long as we end up saving souls. Dad's enthusiasm for travel means that we wash diapers in motels and hang them out the car windows to dry, travel by train at night to save hotel costs, and eat a lot of bologna sandwiches.

A few months earlier, when we were on our way to Minnesota to begin The Preparation for returning to India, the car broke down late in the afternoon as we crossed from California into the Arizona desert. By dusk we despaired of being rescued; not a single vehicle passed by on this deserted highway.

My parents, though, can make the best of about anything. Dad said, "Phyllis, Grace, and Betty, you can sleep in the rack on top of the car. Paul, you help me take the baggage down, quickly, before it gets completely dark. Joanne, you sleep on the front seat of the car; Gwennie, the middle. Margie, you'll be fine in the back." Then he opened up some cots and wedged them between cactus plants, so that he, Mom, and Paul were the most comfortable of all of us, except for the possibility of snakes wandering by, but nobody mentioned them. The three on top of the car spent a sleepless night in fear of falling off. I didn't sleep because of the strangeness of it all. About five in the morning, a friendly truck driver took pity on us, fussed with the engine, and we limped into Flagstaff for permanent repairs.

Now, on this trip we are making the border crossing that our family will later giggle and shake our heads over because it is a doozy. The Minnesota Preparation Period for our return to India is finished and we are returning to California, ready to board the *S.S. Marine Swallow*, the ship that will carry us all the way back to India. The steamer trunks, set up on end on the wooden rack on top of the car, carry the clothes, shoes, and household goods we will need for seven years, although some has been packed in barrels and sent ahead to the San Francisco docks, ready to be loaded onto the ship.

Once again we have been wrenched from our home; once again we have said many goodbyes—this time to our new Minnesota friends, to the faithful church ladies; to uncles, aunts, and cousins; and, most painful of all, to Grandma. She is my rock; her home the place to which I will come should my parents ever forget me in their busy missionarying.

On this trip, with all the bickering, bathroom stops, finding parks in which to eat and rest, and fixing flats and blowouts that average one a day because of the poor quality rubber in war-rationed tires, we cheer loudly when we make more than one hundred miles in one day. For two weeks we squish ourselves into the car and pass the hours by singing all the songs we know, mostly hymns like, "I'm Going Home on the Morning Train," and the German "Nun Ist Sie Erschienen," and "Davundu Prayma," in Telegu. We never tire of Phyllis' stories of a make-believe girl named Mitvesle. Finally, we whoop and holler. "California—40 miles," the sign promises. Almost there!

"Let's keep going," we cry unanimously, invigorated despite the late hour. What do we care? I will soon sleep, draped over Betty's shoulder, and Dad will carry me to bed in some cheap motel down the road—well, if not to bed, then a blanket spread on the floor.

"Should be just a few minutes to pass inspection, and we'll be on our way," Dad promises when the lights of the border check point loom up ahead. We are all so very tired, but Mama is alert enough to remember California's paranoia about people like us bringing in bugs to contaminate their fruit orchards. She gently wakes us, "Hand me all the food. We'll be out of here soon." Always hungry, we've eaten most of it but sleepily search the rubble around us to hand her what little we find. She sorts out the fruit, packs it in a small sack, and stores it by her feet, ready to pass to the inspector. Exhausted, but clearly pleased with her foresight, she relaxes.

"Remind me to give this to the inspector," she says, dozing off.

You need to know Mama. She is tough. She knows how to circle the globe with a passel of children; she can raise a family in a country where the water has to be boiled twice before drinking; and she can kill snakes and keep babies safe from raging bulls, scorpions, typhoid, and lice. Without vomiting, she once treated a woman who kept the worms in her ears quiet by feeding them with leaves. She has endured the heartbreaking pain of sending her offspring to boarding school for ten months of the year, watched her third-born slowly die in her arms with no medical help available, and given solace to lepers. Passing this inspection should be a piece of cake.

"Out of the car!" a uniformed inspector, looking every bit like an army officer, marches up.

"The sack," I whisper to Mama.

She quickly holds up the small sack of fruit. "Here, it's all here," she says. He pushes her arm roughly aside and tells her to keep her mouth shut. Undaunted, she waves it in his arrogant face. Too full of himself to listen, the inspector waves her aside and hollers for us to hurry. Mama tries once more to get his attention, but again he pushes her aside. She gives up. We wearily untangle our entwined bodies, emerge from the car, and slump down on the sidewalk to watch and wait.

If only he had chatted with us for a moment, we would have informed him that we are Mennonites. Everyone knows that Mennonites don't lie, cheat, or steal because lightening will strike, sizzle us like burned bacon, and then straight to Hell, do-not-pass-Go, do-not-collect-two-hundred dollars. Remember Lot's wife? But we don't get the chance. Maybe he thinks sleepy children plot the demise of California orchards, or, as Betty suggests, maybe his wife put too much starch in his uniform.

Please, God, don't let him look up. But he does. "Take down all those trunks," he orders, pointing to the steamer trunks on end on top of the car. Does he know how many men and how many hours it took to hoist those trunks to the roof of the station wagon? He doesn't care; just doing his job. Dad and Paul begin to drag the trunks down, one at a time. The inspector stands by but offers no help while they grunt, sweat, push, and pull. Fortunately for him, Mennonites don't swear. When all the steamer trunks are in a neat row on the ground, Dad finds the keys and lifts the lids to display the clothing, linens, and dishes lovingly packed by the church ladies in Minnesota.

The inspector begins his search. Must be some bug-ridden fruit in here somewhere. He riffles through each trunk, throwing clothing in every direction. When that fails to bring the forbidden fruit to light, he digs down deep, grabs as much of the contents as possible, and dumps it on the ground. Wouldn't the Mennonite ladies who sewed all these garments be dismayed! Several hours later, he struts away, satisfied that we have no contraband hidden anywhere. Mama wearily repacks each trunk; Dad and Paul push, pull, and tug them back up to the rack and tie them down. We stumble into our seats just as the sun is rising.

Numbed by the experience, we slowly drive away. Nobody says a word. Then the silence is broken as Mama laughs hysterically—not a giggle but more like the maniacal laughter of a madman. She can't stop. We try to ask, but she is bent over, tears dripping onto her skirt. I hold my breath. Mama has finally lost it, gone over the edge. She has hit the wall, gone crazy, bonkers. It had to happen sometime. Stunned, we just stare at her. Then, with a triumphant shriek, she slowly raises her arm. Dangling from her fingers is the little brown sack of fruit that remained right there where she left it—by her feet. As giggles and then whoops of laughter ripple through the car, we cross the border into California.

CHAPTER 13

Gift from the Priests

WHILE ALL OTHER American children are slaving away in school, my sisters, brother, and I are truant. We sail out of San Francisco harbor in early December, 1946, with a handful of other missionaries, an assortment of not-so-religious passengers, and a passel of Catholic priests—all bound for the Orient. Some of the California Mennonites have caravanned to see us off. Being of a liberal sort of Mennonite, they are not distinguishable from the Methodist and Presbyterians who also stand on the pier, waving to their loved ones. We gesture and shout until the ship slowly slips from the dock. The gulf between the ship and the shore slowly widens as does our link to our friends and relatives. From this point on, the paths of the Mennonites in America and those of our family will forever take drastically different turns. Even before the shore is completely out of sight, our family is already in a land so foreign to these Mennonites that they will never again know or understand our lives, nor we theirs. Our family is cut off.

Cut off from two sisters as well. Our family wept in pain when we left behind two sisters, Phyllis and Grace, at that Kansas Mennonite college. The last we saw of these sisters was them standing in tight embrace, sobbing. We drove away, waving frantically, even after the car turned the first corner. None of us spoke for a very long time, engulfed in grief beyond words.

Our ship, the *S.S. Marine Swallow*, formerly carried World War II troops to foreign soil and is now poorly disguised as a passenger vessel. This vessel will be our home for the next four weeks as we travel to China, Singapore, and finally Bombay.

The trunks of new clothes sewn so lovingly by the Minnesota church ladies and the new car, a gift from the California Mennonites, reside in the ship's dark, cold hold below deck. My sisters, brother, and I are free to roam and quickly realize that for this brief period of time, we will be suspended between the restraints of the frowning Mennonite preachers on one shore and the stern mission boarding school rules about to constrain us on the other. At sea, Dad gives us his undivided attention, reading aloud, playing shuffle board, and tossing the deck tennis rubber ring on the upper deck. God apparently has given him a short reprieve from work, so we make the most of it.

Cementing friendships with the other children, whose parents are mostly missionaries or employed by some embassy or another, takes about a half an hour, and our shared intentions become clear in about five minutes. Having the run of the ship, we intend to own it. In no time flat, we become acquainted with every deck and galley and learn to hop the raised doorways with latched back iron doors that interrupt the long hallways. We learn the names and country of origin of every crew member, visit the engine rooms below, and observe the captain twirling knobs and scanning the sea ahead. We peek at the non-missionary, worldly adults who are endlessly bent over sinful games of bridge and poker, our first opportunity to examine at close range those Satan-faced cards.

Mother perceives the assignment of our family to a sliver of a stateroom as a gift from God. It even has its very own postage-stamp sized bathroom, and there are enough bunks for all of us, except Paul. He joins the other passengers who are booked into large, multi-bunked staterooms, serving forty or so men or women and dividing parents from each other and sisters from brothers. When the gales rage, we scramble to take refuge in our bunks to avoid injury from our trunks that glide back and forth across the floor with each swell of the waves. Being prone to seasickness, my dashes to the toilet to vomit must be timed according to the tilt of the ship in one direction or the other to avoid being smashed by the careening luggage.

Most enticing to my sisters and me is the forbidden fruit, that of which we have only heard but never witnessed—Catholic priests.

Garbed in black-as-night robes and white-as-snow collars, the twenty or so priests wander about the decks, sometimes bent in prayer with hands grasping beads, other times chattering or simply staring pensively out to sea.

Betty, Joanne, and I eye these priests with rising interest. We sidle closer, glancing over our shoulders for disapproving parents. From the pulpit we have heard of Catholics. "They worship idols; they aren't going to Heaven," is what we're told, but the Mennonite church and condemnatory ministers are far away. Furthermore, Dad is safely ensconced in a deck chair with his Bible, and Mom is washing clothes in the cabin's tiny sink. Now is our chance, our opportunity.

"After all, doesn't Dad encourage us to see the world," I rationalize. "Doesn't he tell us that skating and movies, a sin in America, are not sinful when we are in boarding school?" Bolstered, we give in to temptation.

Watching for an opening, like cowboys separating a calf from its mother, we cut two fairly good-looking but unsuspecting, frocked men from the herd. Betty courageously begins the conversation. Joanne and I hang back a step or two to wait. No lightning bolt, no booming voice from Heaven, no idols swished out from under their robes; God must be on our side.

One of the priests is dark-haired, silent, even shy. So attractive, I think, and so very, very young; not much older than we are. The other is handsome, blond, friendly looking and almost flirty.

"Where are you going?" we burst out.

"To India," the blond responds.

"Just like us!" We are delighted.

"Where are the others going?" emboldened, we push on.

"Well, Father John here is going to get off in Singapore; Father James and Father Matthew are assigned to China. The rest of us are going to India."

"What's your name?" Might as well get to know them.

"Father Francis." And with that our bravado is exhausted; we make a run for safety. But we have so many questions left.

We meet again and again over the next few weeks and relax around these strange and fascinating fellows. I want to ask—but don't—what they wear under those stuffy robes, if they take off that garb and wear pajamas to bed, and won't those robes be too hot in India? I especially would like to have a glimpse of those idols.

Instead, I stick with safe questions, "What about your family? Where do you come from?"

Father Francis is from New York. "I'm from Wisconsin," says Father John.

"What about your family?"

"My parents and my brothers are back there, at home," he says.

"Do you miss them?" My sisters and I can't imagine being without each other, ever.

"Yes, but the Church is my family now," his hand wandering toward his beads.

"Will you be alone on your mission stations?" I envision him in an Indian village, without the comfort of the sisters, brothers, or parents that I have. Father John reassures us that they will be in pairs, and I feel better but am worried about their imminent loneliness, the desolation of boarding school whispering in my ear.

I ask, "How soon will you get to go back? To your family? We get to go to America every seven years." I assume some similarities.

"No," Father John says, sounding sad. "We will never go back; this is for life."

"What do you mean! Never go back?" Betty, Joanne, and I demand in unison.

"Just that. Never. We will stay at our mission posts for the rest of our lives."

"Until you die?"

"Yes, until we die." He smiles a little but doesn't look at us.

What can we say to this? That we are better off? That seven years is forever for us, but forever is truly forever for them? Never see my parents, sisters, brothers, cousins? Never eat ice cream, red apples, cherry pie, or Grandma's pickles? We back away, separated by the very thought of their plight, our friendship now altered. What was similar—leaving family for boarding school in our case and for mission work in theirs—is a bond stretched too far. We now view the priests in a new light; their talk, even their gait as they stride about the decks, seems different, and I begin to view them as brave heroes, even martyrs, their idols forgotten.

In Hong Kong, we and the other passengers gratefully exchange our sea legs for the steadiness of firm soil beneath our feet. Mom barters for trinkets and large carved chests that smell of camphor until the ship's horn blasts for us to return. Then our ship glides through yellow waters where families fish from sampans and little boys dive for coins. Gossip soon spreads that one of the priests has deserted, gone back home, defied his church, his vows. Can you do that? Change your mind? Could we turn around, go back? I think of Dad and know the answer.

Christmas on board a ship is another one of those special treats that our family gets to have, according to Mom. She warns us that gifts will be sparse under these conditions, but there will be festivities, and we hear from Father Francis that there is to be a Christmas Eve Mass said in the recreation room—at midnight.

We appeal to Dad, "Can we go? We've never seen a mass? There's nothing to do here; it's boring. Can't we go, just this once? Wouldn't this be an education for us?" This last is always a trump card to play in emergencies. Dad holds education next to Godliness.

To our delight he says, "Yes." An absent-minded, "Yes," but a "Yes" nevertheless.

Long before midnight, my brother and sisters and I, along with our ship-board friends, are seated at the back, safely away from any magic that might drift from the strangely set table at the front. Red coverings, brass ornaments, incensed globes waved about, statues, Latin chants, wine and wafers—we are mesmerized. Yet we come away unscathed, disproving all Mennonite warnings. The comb, brush, and mirror set smuggled aboard as gifts from our parents pale in comparison to the enchantment of this Christmas Eve Mass.

Long before we dock in Bombay, I begin to suffer waves of desolation. I lie in my bunk, thinking I can drain away in advance some of the inevitable and looming-closer-each-day pain of the parting from Mom and Dad. Once I am deposited at boarding school, I won't see them again until May, such an impossibly long time. I hide my tears so my sisters won't tease me for crying already; we aren't even there yet.

Late one day, after four weeks at sea, the engines slow and tugboats shove us gently against Bombay's large docks. Long before the ropes are tied to the wharf, our family stands at the railing, searching the crowd on the dock for Mr. Dyck, a fellow missionary who is to meet us and squire us off to our mission station for a few days before we are whisked off to school. The gangplank is lowered, and passengers rush to disembark, pushing and shoving as hard as only a month ago they pressed to board the ship. It is as though one moment more on this boat is more than they can possibly endure. Doing the Christian thing, our family waits patiently for our turn, something like "turning the other cheek." I watch the passengers cautiously, yet urgently, make their way down the slanted gangplank, gripping luggage in one hand and the railing in the other.

The crowd momentarily grows quiet, attention arrested by the sight of the long line of priests solemnly stepping down the gangplank, robes flowing, heads held high; their very presence shouting sacrifice. Tears come to my eyes, certain that all that black cloth hides pain worse even than my own. And just then a new thought comes to me, like a bolt of Heaven-sent lightning, maybe prayed up to me from Father Francis, now down on the dock. If these priests can so courageously step onto Indian soil never to return home again, can I not stay in boarding school for only months at a time? I decide right then and there that maybe, just maybe, I can. So I take my sisters' hands, hold my head high, and step toward the gangplank, grateful for this precious gift from the priests.

CHAPTER 14

New Dresses for School

ON MY DRAB, olive-green, army surplus footlocker, in large, white letters is written:

Gwendolyn Hiebert
Kodaikanal School
Kodaikanal, South India

I stare at this label that Dad so carefully painted, a century ago it seems. Yet, it was only a few months ago that we were in Minnesota, on the other side of the globe, getting ready for this day when I must unpack this trunk here in my dormitory. Even the mission station at Mahbubnager, where Mom and Dad are saving souls, seems far away.

To get to school, it took three days and two nights by train for Paul, Betty, Joanne, and me to get to Madurai at the foothills of the Palni Hills. Following that, we took a bouncy ride up the *ghat* on a rickety bus. I was fascinated by the faintly familiar sights on the dusty ride up the mountain: the long, thin, silvery trail of water cascading down Rat Tail Falls; coolies balancing oversized loads on their heads; oxen blocking our passage as they laboriously hauled their carts up the steep inclines; horns blasting, warning the presence of vehicles headed straight for us as we careened around bends; drivers shouting to one another; and, half-way up, the same old man beside the same mud hut beckoning travelers to stop for tea—and a quick and careful squat behind a bush if necessary.

Arriving at the school compound, the other students and I tumbled wearily from the bus, dirty with dust from the roads and soot from the coal burning train. I, like some, held back; others cheered and rushed to greet friends as though they had been parted for years instead of a few months. Coolies quickly climbed to the roof of the bus to retrieve our luggage, sorting it out from the baskets of chickens, bundles bound in rags, and suitcases held together by flimsy ropes. The principal stood by, calmly directing coolies, and pointing us in the direction of our various dormitories. My sisters and I trudged up the long hill, past the gym, the classroom-lined quadrangle, the cafeteria, and finally down a steep, covered walkway to Boyer Hall, the girl's dormitory.

The matron, a large, no-nonsense woman, marched us to our rooms. "Upstairs for little girls, downstairs for high school girls. Don't let me catch you downstairs," she said, frowning and wagging her finger at Joanne and me. The first of her many rules, this one let me know that my access to my sister Betty is going to be limited. I panicked. Who will help me fix my hair? Help me with homework? Worry about me as she always does?

Joanne and I, along with five other girls, were quickly assigned to a large room near the end of the hall, home for the next ten months. The matron barked, "Your trunks are by your beds. Get unpacked before dinner. The first bell means wash your hands, the second go for supper, and don't be late." She stomped down the hall, without a "Happy to see you" or "If you need anything, let me know." No hugs, for sure. I guess sixty homesick girls are too much for anyone to handle, even if called by God to be a matron.

I stare down at my trunk. The moment has arrived when, finally, I can bring to light all those clothes sewn by the Minnesota church ladies, garments that have been snuggled down inside this trunk all this while, clothes that, until now, I could gaze upon but not wear. I have pictured this moment ever since I watched them fashioned from cotton, wool, and corduroy, the fabric sporting plaids, polka dots, or flowers, all adorned with laces, ribbons, bright buttons, and ruffles.

Opening the trunk, I pull out the plaid, pleated skirt and jacket made just for me by Mrs. Thiessen. I press the skirt to my face; it still smells of Grandma's house and, just like that, I am back there with the aromas, the noises, and the presence of all those kind ladies. I remember how unusually still the house was in the late afternoons after the church women laid aside their needles and left. Then Grandma would doze in her rocker while Mama took the opportunity to rest in her room. It was then that Joanne and I could steal into the front parlor, and, in the dusk, finger the garments, so new and ever so fine. "One day," I had promised Joanne, "we will wear these. We'll be so grand!"

My supply of cousin Lois's hand-me-downs were quite lovely, but when those Minnesota children teased me for wearing them, I wished they knew about these clothes so carefully packed away in my green army trunk.

"Tha-a-at's Lois' old dre-e-ss," those classmates often chanted as I walked to and from school, Lois at my side. In the classroom, they poked each other and giggled, whispering behind their hands. "Why are you wearing Lois' clothes? Don't you have any?" one girl demanded. I didn't let myself cry until I was almost home, and they were out of sight. Bursting into Grandma's house, I hugged My Last Doll Peggy—last because "You're getting too old for dolls," my parents had said, so I picked her myself from *The Sears and Roebuck Catalog*. Cradling Peggy, I sat down on my footlocker and rubbed my hand over the white letters, Gwendolyn Hiebert. The clothes inside were mine. I wanted to say, "Tease me all you like, but nobody can take these pretty dresses away from me. Nobody."

"Bell's going to ring," Joanne brings me abruptly back, "she's going to be mad." So we begin to unpack. Peggy, out first, goes on my bed. Then I hold up the red plaid skirt and matching jacket, my favorite, and then the rest, one after another, all to be hung in my share of the small wardrobe standing along one wall. At the sight of this abundance of new clothes, our roommates fall silent. Their trunks hold mostly hand-me-downs of hand-me downs because these girls haven't been on furlough to America for a long, long time. Our un-packing is like watching someone else's Christmas.

"O-o-oh," and a long, drawn out, "Ah-h-h," and, "Can I feel that?" is all the roommates need to say to remind me of my Minnesota tor-menters. The tables have turned; I like being envied. Magnanimous now, I invite them to share. Forgetting the bell, we try on first one piece of glory and then another. We giggle with delight as we strut about, admiring ourselves and each other in this abundance of finery.

"Ding-a-ling," the bell catches us by surprise. We scramble to wash up and skip to the dining hall, hand-in-hand, our spirits lifted and faces reflecting the magic of the church-ladies, fine dresses.

"Friends," I think, "I have friends!"

The news spreads quickly. The next afternoon when school is out, my roommates and I escape our classrooms and race to the dormitory.

"Let's go!" we shout. Joanne, the fleetest, runs ahead and almost collides with the matron, who is standing, arms crossed, in the door-way. Joanne skids to a stop. The rest of us crowd behind her, quickly subdued.

"Girls," the no-nonsense matron says sternly to Joanne and me, "Six dresses will be sufficient for this school year. One for Sunday, five for weekdays. I have selected the most practical. The rest have already been packed in your trunks and taken to storage."

I rush to the closet. My red plaid skirt and jacket are still there. "For Sundays," barks the matron and clomps down the hall.

I wrap the plaid skirt around Peggy and place her by my pillow, ready to comfort me when I will cry myself to sleep tonight. "I'll sew and sew and make you all the beautiful clothes you want," I whisper to my doll. And I do—elegant gowns, dresses, pajamas, and even hand-knit sweaters, just as pretty as the clothes now stashed away in storage.

Off to School: Waiting for the Train

CHAPTER 15
The Power of Bubble Gum

I HATE BOARDING school! Most nights I slip into Joanne's narrow, single bed for comfort to ease the homesickness that invariably falls over me like a shroud after lights out. Then there are the rules and the high stone walls surrounding the compound that confines us. No trips to the bazaar without a chaperone; no journeys to the bathroom after lights out; communal showers three times a week; get up to the bell; go to breakfast to the bell, change classes to the bell, four o'clock tea at the bell, supper at the bell; and then study hall until 9:30 every night, including Friday. Eat what they serve, like oatmeal with weevils in it. Sunday night is toast topped with scrambled eggs and spinach globbed on top, so I make sure to wear a dress with pockets into which I can hide the spinach and hope the teachers won't notice the drip down my legs that ends in green splatters on the floor. We students have a song in honor of the food:

There is a boarding school five miles away
Where they serve rotten eggs, five times a day.
Oh, how the children yell when they hear the dinner bell;
Oh, how the eggs do smell, five times a day.

I love boarding school! Day and night I get to be with my friends; no "You can't have a friend over today," or "It's your turn to wash dishes, Gwennie," or "But they aren't Menonnite, not One of Us." This school happily accepts Methodists, Presbyterians, Lutherans, and even a few whose parents are not missionaries but work for the government or large companies. Every night has slumber party potential, and studies are endurable because the tall eucalyptus and pine trees promise relief in the form of hikes and camping trips.

"Time to vote," our class president says at our weekly meeting. "Where do we want to go camping next month?"

"A leopard was spotted at Poombari," says John. "Let's go there!" It's unanimous; we thrill at the risk. Besides, Poombari is only twelve miles away, an easy hike. Then the class decides on a Saturday event— a ten-mile hike before breakfast, an evening roller skating party in the gym, a taffy pull, or a buffalo steak roast over an open fire.

At Sunday night vespers, students sit on the floor and sing hymns that remind me so much of home that I choke up. However, I promptly forget my parents during the three-mile walk around the lake that follows where cow patties are strewn like land mines lying in wait for couples too engrossed to watch their step. The yearly competition between the Blue and the Gold on Field Day engenders fierce, year-long loyalty to one's team. Movies arrive from America twice a month, sometimes starring Jeanette McDonald and Nelson Eddie, who keep me awake at night, dreaming of the day when I too shall fall gloriously in love.

Most important, though, are my friends. All abandoned by parents who zealously toil to save souls on the hot Indian plains, we must comfort, nurture, and love one another lest that emptiness in the pit of our stomachs grows to an unmanageable size.

We care for each other instinctively. Once Mom and Dad remember my birthday and send money for me to invite six friends to a birthday party at tea time. But there are twelve girls in my class! Sitting cross-legged on the grass beneath the giant stride, we solemnly resolve that all will attend, but each is to take only half a portion of cake, IJ (Indian junk—like cereal peppered with hot spices), and strong tea turned muddy-white with boiled milk and *jaggery* (brown sugar that comes in a hard, round ball).

Our friendships remain strong even if one finds a package from America on her bed which, by the way, never, ever, happens to me. When one of these Fortunate Girls in our seven-bed room receives a package, we crowd onto her bed, "ooh" and "aah," sniff, feel, and exclaim over every treasure pulled from the box sent by a relative or family friend and costs more money to mail than we can imagine anyone spending on us. Even a postage stamp for a letter sent regular mail to the States—which takes three months to arrive—is more than I am willing to humble myself and beg for from Dad. So I don't write, and my former friends in America probably think I drowned on the ship coming over, was eaten by tigers, or died of snake-bite.

On the rare occasion when a Fortunate Girl receives a package from America, its arrival causes considerable excitement, and we begin to view her in a new light. Up to this point, she has been just one of us with the usual flaws and an occasional talent, nothing of which to take particular notice. But now she seems somehow different, something like a movie star. I search for that quality in the Fortunate Girl that is so special that someone in America would remember her, know her name, spend the money for gifts, package them, and pay the enormous postage. I am astonished that this could happen but finally conclude that Methodists and Presbyterians can allow themselves to care more because they have smaller families.

On one of these rare, package-receiving days, the Fortunate Girl's roommates and her best friends from across the hall push and shove onto her bed. Anticipation runs high. First we examine the myriad stamps pasted all over the top and cry, "Open it!" Out comes the usual candy, a blouse, underwear, and even comic books, which I am not supposed to read but do because Mom and Dad are too far away to find out, and Joanne won't tell. Scattered in the bottom of this package are little yellow and blue square-shaped bits with bold lettering—bubble gum. What is this? We have never seen bubble gum. Chewing gum is precious stuff that comes in sticks, is gray, and costs lots of money, even a nickel sometimes, but they don't have it in India except maybe at Spencers, but that is about five blocks away in the bazaar off the compound, and persuading a teacher to chaperone such an excursion is as likely as saving a *rupee* to spend on gum, my allowance being only two *annas* a week. In America, Joanne, with whom I share a bed, wakes up in the morning yelling, "Mom, she did it again!" Mom sends Phyllis to cut my yesterday's chewing gum out of Joanne's hair. Joanne is mad at me, I am mad at losing my treasured gum; and who knows when a church lady will give me another nickel.

When this first shipment of bubble gum arrives, we pass one of the pink globules around to be squeezed, examined, and sniffed, puzzled that these pieces of gum seem so much larger than one small stick of Spearmint or Juicy Fruit. When the Fortunate Girl pops one in her mouth and chews ever so slowly, her cheeks puff out like she has the mumps. Encircling her, our heads touch as we lean forward, intent on her every chew. Our jaws vicariously move with hers. She moves the wad around in her mouth and then slowly and carefully works the gum over her front teeth and blows; must be instinctive, like burping. A bubble forms on her lips. Our empty mouths produce nothing. She blows harder, but the bubble pops. "O-o-oh," we sigh, then cry, "Let me try," already certain we can do it better. So, magnanimously, the Fortunate Girl allows each of us a turn with that first piece of gum, passing it around until everyone is satisfied that she too can blow bubbles. The flavor disappears but not the gum's elasticity.

We solemnly eye the remaining pieces of gum and look questioningly at the Fortunate Girl; we now face the truest test of our friendship. Who will get to chew them all? Will she share? She will. Together we make what is deemed a fair decision, one that stands for years to come. The Fortunate Girl will make a list of all her friends in the order of her fondness for them, her best friend being first and least favorite being last. After the Fortunate Girl has chewed each piece, it will go to the girl who is first on the list. When she has chewed the gum sufficiently, she is to pass it to the girl whose name is next on the list. When that girl has chewed it for an appropriate amount of time, she will pass it on to girl whose name is next, and so on. Separate lists are constructed for each piece of gum with names slightly rearranged so that our names appear higher or lower, depending on the wad. I am never first in line but occasionally make it to third or fourth, which translates to week three or four of the gum's life.

The care and keeping of each piece of gum weighs heavily on our minds. If we leave the wads on a dresser top, the servants or a girl not on The List might steal it. If we take it to class, we risk the cruelty of having to spit it into the waste basket. In class, I watch as John sticks his behind his ear, but that is repugnant; anyway, it would stick in our long hair. We finally conclude that the only safe hiding place is beneath the current user's pillow, and any thief will be ostracized by all of us, the very worst possible thing that can happen to anyone in boarding school. The plan works as do our letters of thanks—sowing the seeds as the Bible commands. We reap a harvest of bubble gum. From then on, precious pink gum arrives in almost every package from across the seas.

Relationships among us begin to take on new meaning with the advent of bubble gum. We never know who the next Fortunate Girl will be, so staying on good terms becomes essential to one's relative standing on the bubble gum list. I try passing wicked gossip around about those whose names most frequently appear at the top of the lists, but it takes considerable effort to keep such fires turned away from myself. Staying on good terms is by far the wisest route to take.

So that is the story. Over the years, in that dreadful but wonderful boarding school, it turns out that it is from bubble gum, not from what our fathers preach from their pulpits, that we learn the value of being kind and good. Strife and anger serve to bump us down on the list; sharing, compassion, and praise are in our best interests. On the other hand, neither we nor our unsuspecting parents ever figure out that bubble gum was the number one contributor to the rapid spreading of mumps that spring—maybe the lice too.

Thus, despite all the ups and downs of dormitory life in India, in the end, it is the bubble gum, together with our desperate need for affection, which cements our relationships. One should never, ever, underestimate the power of bubble gum.

The Giant Stride

CHAPTER 16
Pranks and Other Useful Sports

- *Reflection provided by my older sister Betty*

To the Reader:

While the tales of students' adventures at the boarding school here in Kodaikanal, South India, are told from my sister Gwen's perspective, the stories may be digested more easily with a bit of historical background and an understanding of the circumstances surrounding these escapades. The following is provided not as an excuse for our behavior but rather as an explanation for what was and is now, at the telling of this story, occurring at this school. Sincerely,

Elizabeth (Betty) Hiebert

FROM LATE IN the 19th until the middle of the 20th century, American, German, English, and Canadian missionaries—doctors, nurses, preachers, and teachers—flocked to India with great zeal, eager to convert the poverty stricken to Christianity, hoping to save their own souls in the process. While these missionaries busily built hospitals and schools and traveled by car, ox cart, or even by foot to the remotest of villages to teach and preach, their own children were packed off to the hills to attend boarding schools, there being no English schools yet available in the hot plains where the missionaries toiled for God.

These missionaries undoubtedly assuaged their guilt over abandoning their children to the care and keeping of others by envisioning Kodaikanal School in the hills of South India as a place where house parents lovingly wiped tears from youngsters' eyes, read the little ones bedtime stories, and kissed the darlings goodnight while tucking them in bed, even offering cocoa and cookies to stave off hunger that might overtake the precious children before breakfast. Most likely included in this utopia were teachers who affectionately put their arms around students when they failed and celebrated successes with warm smiles and praise, teachers who never raised their voices or spoke an unkind word. The parents' delusions likely included happy thoughts of their children alternately studying, eating, and sleeping, with a few moments of play, even hiking the hills a little here and there in between; why else the requirement of sturdy shoes and camping gear? The missionaries might even have persuaded themselves that they were doing their children a great favor by bestowing on them not only the best in education and clean, cool mountain air but love and kindness from not just two parents but a host of adults who cared deeply for their offspring.

We, the children, do little to deprive our parents of their hallucinations. We can handle boarding school ourselves, we are certain. Yet the reality of our experience at this school is a bit different from these parental fantasies. We do receive an A-plus education; we do pile our plates high with curry and rice at noon. We actually study long hours in the evenings, including Friday nights, and invigorated by our hiking and the pure, cool mountain air, we regularly sleep eight hours at night. But during moments stolen at lunch, dinner, four o'clock tea, the longer stretches between tea and dinner, and even greater periods on weekends, we become creative in our plans to apply pressure to the bonds placed on us by those we view not as loving substitute parents but as our captors. For us, the multitude of rules, the compound walls beyond which we must not stray, the mounds of homework, the restrictions on how many servings of curry we may have at lunch, the evening meals of watery soup, and bedtime snacks provided by food stealthily transferred from the dinner table to our rooms or from care-packages from America, or even cans of cooked sweetened condensed milk bought with saved-up allowances, all cause us to feel somewhat rebellious.

For our young spirits, entertainment and rebellion are rolled into one and are as essential to our survival as the air we breathe, a state of affairs that has undoubtedly existed since the inception of this school. Consequently, we conjure, refine, reject, and finally accept the choicest plots, and parties are recruited to execute the devilish deeds. The final step is to set precise timetables to ensure success. Planning is as delicious as enacting, so that even temporarily placing a particularly brilliant plan on a back burner is just an opportunity to savor it, much as we savor our short supply of bubblegum.

The executed offenses can be categorized not by their depth of sinfulness but by whether or not the culprits get caught. The first category: "Doing the Deed and Getting Caught." These wrong-doings, while numerous, do not receive as much admiration as the second category: "Doing the Deed and Not Getting Caught." Each transgression is worthy in its own right and considered fruit for much analysis following completion, regardless of the category.

The Getting Caught category is large. My younger sister Gwen (she no longer wants to be called Gwennie, so I must respect that) tells me that when she sneaks across the hall after lights out and climbs into bed with her friend Eleanor in order to whisper and giggle, the housemother, whose hearing is keener than that of a hunting dog, stands with arms crossed and commands her back to her own bed. On occasion, even I am involved in some mild pranks. Once I helped my roommates let down the rope ladder from our second story room, intending to take a late night romp about the campus. When Francie climbed down, I whispered, "Are you down yet?" Principal Papa Phelps replied, "Yes, I do believe so." When the boys periodically set off hidden alarm clocks in the library during study hall, they are easily identified by the names stenciled on their property. Gwen's classmates Paul and Bill went camping once and were frightened by a tiger during the night, so they drove it away and survived unharmed. Instead of praise, they found themselves in the principal's office, facing a very angry rajah who claimed the hooligans chased away a tiger he had hoped to catch, having tied up a goat for bait. When Eddie, Floyd, and Bill, also from Gwen's class, took an after-lights-out stroll around the lake in their pajamas, they were caught by the music teacher. Love notes passed back and forth in class are usually confiscated and read aloud by the teacher. Someone snitched, and the rules were tightened when a girl was smuggled into the boys' dormitory. The list of sins is endless but certainly not discouraging. The addiction to sin is not hampered by losses. Akin to that of Las Vegas' most ardent gamblers, our obsession is easily fed by intermittent successes.

"Doing the Deed and Not Getting Caught" earns high esteem, even envy. Without detection, almost everyone at one time or another escapes the compound, particularly at night, just to boat across the lake or maybe to walk the three miles around it. Some make secret purchases in the bazaar or rendezvous with their latest True Love at Fairy Falls or Bear Shola. My friend Roger regularly begs *"baksheesh"* from the halva vendor right outside the compound and receives a sliver of the sweet for his effort. (Many years later, when he returns to find the very same halva man much older but still plying his trade, Roger will press into the man's palm a substantial number of *rupees* as a belated thanks.)

Gwen confides in me that she frequently skips piano practice in order to scheme with her friend Margaret. These two put frogs in a roommate's bed, but when the roommate sat down, she squished the frogs. Girls in this school frequently feign illness and win a few days vacation in the "dishpan" (the school's dispensary). My friends and I discover that when we hang our heads over the side of the bed, count to 50, and stand up suddenly, the result is a dead faint. The boys regularly put pins in the cords of study hall lights to blow the fuses and delay the evening ritual of preparing for the next days' classes. Without detection, the boys use their binoculars to spy on girls clad only in swimsuits, catching a few minutes of sun on the mountain slopes across the lake. Once David, John, and Delmar, well known for their pranks, threw rocks over the side of the mountain at Coker's Walk, but, thankfully, the death of a sacred cow below was not attributed to their actions. John and his buddies sometimes sneak a skinny dip in the Catholic Seminary's pool—no wet clothes, no suspicion. When Jeanette McDonald and Nelson Eddie sing their love songs during the twice monthly movies, my friends and I take advantage of the dark to hold hands with our current love. The boys occasionally sneak down to the boathouse to set a few punts free. Later, they enjoy the owner's payment and many thanks and *salaams* when the boys graciously offer to retrieve the boats. And so it goes, we sin, we get caught—or not—but, undaunted and considerably proud of ourselves, we thrive.

Yet there is one more category, one which is almost impossible to attain, so impossible it haunts our dreams but is rarely discussed. This feat is "Committing the Sin, Not Getting Caught, AND Receiving Praise." This level is so difficult to achieve that only once, as far as I know, did it occur. With great reverence, the telling of it is passed down from one generation of students to the next, never failing to receive the O-o-hs and A-h-hs the story and its hero deserve. The doer of this deed was not one of those big boys in Block Dormitory, high school fellows with years of experience at conjuring criminal acts that have earned them the awe and admiration of the entire student body. No, this level of achievement was reached by a lad so young he resided in Kennedy Hall that houses only the little schoolboys. This particular boy was not devious and cunning but a clever chap who was able to think quickly, on his feet or off, as it turned out. The story went like this.

One evening after lights out, John invited his closest friends to gather in his room to engage in a time-honored contest—climbing on the dresser, leaping into the air to touch the ceiling, and landing—without breaking a limb—on John's bed. Over and over again, the young boys took turns, some reaching the ceiling with their finger tips, others claiming to do so despite protests to the contrary. As the contest grew more and more intense, the boys became less and less secretive, so that their whispers, hisses, and laughter finally caught the attention of the housemother in her apartment down the hall. So engrossed were the boys in their rush to soar higher and higher that they forgot her proximity. Just as she stealthily made her way toward the uproar, John was perched on the dresser, next in line and quite certain that his long legs could take him to heights that would out-do all others'. He squatted and then sprang. Just at that moment, when his head was so close to the ceiling that he could not only touch it but could place his hands flat enough to leave fingerprints, his spirits already soaring in victory, he glimpsed the slow turning of the door knob. In a flash he knew what was about to transpire. The door would open, the matron would enter, and the next moments, hours, even days, would become his worst nightmare. A visit to the principal's office would precipitate letters home; worse yet, visits to the bazaar, hiking, camping trips, and maybe even tea time would all evaporate for months to come.

This awareness exploded across his brain like a meteor hitting the earth at full speed. John was a very smart boy, and his instincts were keen. He straightened his body in mid-air, and rather than landing in the usual crouching position, he landed so that his feet fell at the foot end of the bed, and his head rested on his pillow. All John had to do was cross his hands over his heart and close his eyes. What the matron saw as she opened the door was not John bouncing on the rumpled bed but a room full of pajama-clad, sweaty, little boys, some racing toward the dresser, some poised on top of the dresser—and John angelically asleep in his bed.

"Boys, get back to your own rooms," roared the matron, "Not asleep? Out of your rooms? Jumping on beds? After lights out? We'll just see what the principal has to say about this in the morning!" Then pointing to John, she said firmly, "You should take a lesson from John. He's a good boy. He's asleep in his own bed."

KODAI SCHOOL

CHAPTER 17
Going to Town

WE MARK OFF the October days—28th, 29th, 30th. Finally on the 31st, all the other students and I are seated precariously on rickety buses that hurl down the mountain to Majurai where we will catch one train or another and scatter. Going home at last. We sing, chant, shout for joy, and poke our heads out windows with glass broken out. We have waited for this day since January, when the old buses labored up the mountain to deposit us at boarding school.

Once home on the mission station, my sisters, brother, and I are happy to be with Mom and Dad every single day. We are lazy, having few chores to do as Dad has hired numerous students to earn their tuition by making our beds, cleaning the house, and serving our meals. At night we are tucked safely into beds with netting tucked in all around to ward off malaria-carrying mosquitoes. In the evenings, we fight for space around a few lanterns and read.

"Too many; what am I to do with them all?" Mom objects each time Dad presents her with a Willing Worker eager to attend his school. "Besides, we just can't afford the servants we already have," she says as hired workers are paid not from the Mission Board's meager allowance but from Dad's salary. Yet, in order to be free to Do God's Work, missionaries' households require a cook, a *mali* to tend the garden, a man to draw water from the well, and a sweeper, the woman who sweeps the house and empties our chamber pots twice a day.

"Just this one," Dad says, "Surely you can find something for this one to do around the house."

When the count reaches about sixteen, she puts her foot down. "Not another one!" And there isn't, until the next time.

With little to do, my sisters, brother, and I read and reread all thirty-seven books in the bookshelf and the old Readers Digests dating back to the early 1900s. The books' edges are frayed because rats prefer to nest among them; their gnawing keeps us awake at night. Soon bored, though, we seek activity. Bribes and whining persuade Paul to accompany Joanne and me on bike rides outside the mission compound, off limits to unaccompanied girls. We play endless games of Monopoly, and I sew or help Mom dispense medicines on the veranda in the afternoons. I miss my friends and write to them, even mailing some when I summon the courage to interrupt Dad's work to ask for stamps.

We look forward to Christmas, though it doesn't feel like a real Christmas when we sleep on the upstairs veranda to escape the indoor heat and palm branches become our Christmas tree. It is the Yearly Conference that truly breaks the monotony. For this event, all the Mennonite families must travel from their lonely mission stations to gather for prayer and write reports to the Mission Board in America in whose hands our fate always rests. All the women missionaries are called Aunties, the men Uncles, and the Indians are "The People." Dad might say, "God sent us here to save The People," or direct a servant to "Gather The People for a meeting." Mom might say, "Uncle and Auntie Wiebe are coming to visit next week," or "Auntie Lorenz is ill, I must go and help." Once when we arrived in New York on furlough, Paul, a small child at the time, was puzzled by the fact that there were so many Aunties and Uncles walking about. "Where are The People?" he asked, expecting the familiar ratio of black to white faces on the street.

The long months that missionaries spend on isolated mission stations create a great need for social interaction, and the coming together at Conference is so sweet that the women hug, chatter, and hug again. The men slap each other on the back and huddle in deep conversation, not wanting to get down to business. For us children, it means four days of freedom with only *ayamas* to watch over us. We ride horses, climb wide spreading banyan trees, wade in nearby muddy streams, throw stones at wild dogs, and write dramas to be enacted for the Aunties and Uncles in the evening. The single ladies— the nurses and school teachers—along with Uncle and Auntie Lorenz who have no children, fuss over us and distribute pop corn and candy special ordered from America months ago. This is our real Christmas!

Between Conference and Christmas, though, we are restless, bored, and want to be with our friends who are at their homes with their parents and are also bored. So we perk up when Dad occasionally announces a shopping trip to Hyderabad City, almost the size of Madras but only forty miles but four hours away. Up at dawn without complaint, we bump along the washboard dirt roads, and cling to our *topees* (pith helmets) as we hang out the windows to feel the rush of air on our faces and wave merrily at the women carrying bundles of sticks on their heads and to those fortunate enough to ride in ox carts. We look past the few filthy beggars sitting by the side of the road. Their hair is matted, flies feed on their open sores, and their weary, sad eyes simply stare at us. They quickly cover their faces with their rags to ward off the unwelcomed swirls of dust our tires stir up.

People are busy washing their clothes and bathing in the river at the edge of the city. We turn solemn when we spot groups of mourners sitting beside the smoking funeral pyres which will still smolder and glow in the moonlight on our way home. Betty dramatically recounts tales from the old days of *sati* when wives were expected to throw themselves atop the pyre to burn alongside their dead husbands or had their heads shaved and were sent to live in poverty with other widows in an ashram, no matter their age.

"Yes," Mom confirms Betty's story, "Hindus used to believe that a wife could help her husband gain spiritual salvation that way; she was thought of as a goddess for dying like that. But that's in the past." She sighs, "Widows have a hard time; nobody seems to want them."

We park, and Dad pays a young boy two *annas* to watch the car, two more to be paid upon our return. Taking Paul's hand, he rushes off to attend to important business in government buildings. This is the best part of the excursion because Mom, my sisters, and I are now free to wander the bazaars to fill Mom's long shopping list. Mom takes her time, stopping to chat with vendors who are as eager to show their wares as she is to see them.

"How is your family?" she begins with the fabric merchant.

"Very good, very good," responds the shopkeeper. "My wife just gave birth to a boy," he says proudly. So mother congratulates him and inquires about the health of the mother and child.

We sit down on the clean white sheet laid carefully across the floor, and a small girl brings us little glasses of hot tea laced with *jaggery* (brown sugar) and tinned milk.

"What would you like to see? A piece of this fine red cloth? Something in blue with gold trim? Whatever you like," and he pulls one bolt of fabric after another from the shelves, scattering the cloth across the floor. After she selects an item, it must be bargained for. Mom enjoys exercising her bartering skills, and the shop keepers delight in the contest. Thus it goes from one shop to another.

Wandering about, we make way for lorries packed so full that people hang on to the sides and even sit on top where they cling for dear life to baskets of chickens and bundles bound with rags or worn rope. We dodge the cars, rickshaws, and bicycles; we make way for camels, cattle, and horses that haul large, overloaded carts. We try to stay clear of the dogs sniffing at garbage and cows that amble, eat, and sleep as they please. We look away from the pitiful souls with elephantitis whose limbs are spread broad and flat across an entire sidewalk and try not to touch the blotched-faced lepers who are missing noses and fingers. All the while, we carefully dodge the steamy cow patties and human waste lying about. In contrast, like blood red, dandelion yellow, sky blue, and burgundy flowers blooming in a drab hay field, women in brightly colored, neatly pleated *saris* make their way gracefully through the throngs, swaying slightly to maintain the large bundles on their heads; their shiny coconut-oiled, black braids that snake down their backs swing in rhythm to their gait.

Unlike the quiet mission compound, here horns blare, shopkeepers and hawkers shout their wares, and bikers twitch their bells in a continuous ding-a-linging—all against a background of high, whining Indian music. Beggars tug at our skirts, whimpering, "*Baksheesh, baksheesh,*" and children paid by shopkeepers entice us with, "Best price, cheap, what you want?"

Even the smells are more pungent here than at home. Best in the world smells waft from curries spiced with cinnamon, cardamom, garlic, cumin, and coriander kept hot by fires fueled with dried manure. To this mixture of odors is added that of dust, chewed and spat beetle nut, urine, sweat, and rotting garbage.

Lunch is a picnic in a park with one can of tinned meat shared 'round, especially bought for this occasion. The day ends at the market where we buy sweet *hulva* for dessert. The final stop is a ritual visit to Helen's grave. Long before I was born—after Paul, but before Betty—our sister, Helen, was a happy baby one day but dead of a high fever the next. The doctor was four hours away from the mission station, too far to go for help, but not too far for burial in the city after she turned cold.

That ends the day in town. We drive home in the darkness and, despite the washboard roads, I fall asleep, but wake when Dad carries me to bed—a rare, and much savored moment alone with my father.

Sometimes Mom and Dad go to town and leave my sisters, brother, and me alone with the servants. These are not good days. Once I fell ill after they left, and by the time they returned at midnight, I was delirious, talking gibberish. At this, my mother stood erect at the foot of my bed and threatened, "If you keep talking like that, I'll call the doctor!" A native doctor resides in a nearby village, but we can't possibly bother anyone at midnight. Dying will have to wait until morning. I survive.

One day the tedium of life on the plains is temporarily broken when Aaron, our cook, proudly announces that his wife has given birth to triplets. Aaron struts around the kitchen, tying and untying his *dhoti*, proud of having sons rather than daughters who require dowries. But, only hours later, he stands at the door, wringing his hands, and sobbing. One little boy has died. Mother cries, saying, "Just like Helen, just like her," and mournfully goes to supply some burial clothes and cloth to line the tiny, quickly constructed casket.

Dismayed at Mom's tears, I ask Betty and Joanne, "What can we do?" The last time we saw her cry was when we left Phyllis and Grace behind, in Kansas. We can't think of anything, so we just tiptoe about and talk in whispers. Late in the day, our family joins the local congregation of Christians in a short trek to the cemetery outside the compound where a grave has been dug deep enough to keep the little body safe from hungry jackals.

A few days later, Mom and Dad go to town, taking baby Margaret with them. Betty, Paul, Joanne, and I are left alone. The day drags on. I sew, read, and pick a fight with Joanne. Then Aaron stands at the door again, sobbing. I don't want to hear that another triplet has died; Mom isn't home. But he has, and Aaron wants to know if one of us will sew a gown for the baby. Betty volunteers my services. I protest; I sew doll clothes and dresses for myself, but not burial gowns for babies.

"Pretend it is for your doll," Betty tries to sooth me. So I hunt for some white cotton, and sew a tiny dress for a little, dead baby and gather fabric for the coffin.

It is dusk before Aaron knocks. The carpenter has completed the casket, and will I do the family the honor of bringing the dress to his hut myself? My feet drag as I follow him on the dusty path across the compound. I do not want to do this. Inside the small, one-room hut lies Aaron's wife with the last little boy cuddled against her; this one must live. She points to a small table on which the lifeless body lies and asks me to dress the baby as a favor to her. The family agrees; this is a fitting tribute to my efforts. I can't; fungus is already growing in the child's mouth and the body is stiff, even more rigid than my doll. Aaron helps me pull the dress over the baby's head, wrestle the stiff arms into the sleeves, and smooth the skirt around his dead feet. I bow, my palms pressed together. "*Salaam,*" I say and rush for home.

The moon is high before the arrangements are completed, but the body must be buried that same day because of the heat. Carrying lanterns, Paul, Betty, Joanne, and I walk single file down the road to the cemetery, Aaron leading the way with the little casket balanced on his head. Our shadows dance eerily beside us. We become still as the preacher talks of Heaven. The women wail, beat their breasts, and the casket is lowered and covered with dirt. We trudge home, the weight of the event so heavy we can't speak. I am too sick at heart to sleep. Why do Mom and Dad have to leave us alone?

I hear the car at midnight. Mom tiptoes up the stairs to check on us. I pull back the mosquito netting, put my arms out and hug her tight. "Please, don't ever leave me again!" I plead, but can't tell her of the dead body, dressing it, and burying it in the dreadful darkness.

"Sh-h-h," she tries to sooth me. She has heard about the baby, "It's okay; it's okay." But down in a dark, hidden part of myself I know—and she knows that I know, but we don't say—that here in India Mom and Dad can go to town in the morning when I am well and perfectly healthy, but I can get sick, die, and be buried before they even get home again. This, we know, is the life of the missionary; this is how we live.

CHAPTER 18

Civil War

"QUIET!" DAD SHOUTS as he pounds on the table, a signal for us to stop arguing, nudging, pointing fingers, and glaring at each other. Captive at the dinner table this particular evening, my sisters, brother, and I, are still home for the holidays and are bored with each other. "There's a real war going on out there; pay attention. You need to know what's going on; history is happening right now, right here under our noses." As fervent as he is about saving souls, so Dad is when it comes to history. He drags our family to places like the Golconda Fort in the nearby hills. In Hyderabad City, we have frequently driven through the Charminar archway, an ancient 1500s monument with magnificent minarets, and visited the Paigah Tombs. We always crane our necks to catch a glimpse of the wealthy Nizam of Hyderabad as he passes through the city on some important business or another.

"Is it true," my sisters and I have asked many times, "true that the Nizam has truck loads of pearls? That he is the richest man in the world? Is he?"

"That's what they say," Dad replies. "But Gandhi, that's who you need to pay attention to now," Dad continues, letting his curry get cold, "you need to know about Gandhi." Dad the Preacher turns Dad the Teacher. Being the only source of news from the world outside our compound walls, Dad takes it upon himself to keep us up to date. "Gandhi is turning India upside down." He takes us back to the beginning. "Gandhi was born in Gujarat, way back in 1869." Grinning, Dad looks at me, "Gandhi had an arranged marriage when he was only thirteen, his bride even younger. About your age, Gwennie." I wonder what it would be like to be married rather than being shipped off to boarding school. I remember a young couple that once came to our bungalow to show us their newborn daughter, boasting that the baby had just been married to a twenty-year-old man. Maybe Gandhi's wife was relieved not to become an old maid.

The servants clear the table while Dad continues. He tells how Gandhi went to London to study law and then lived in Africa where he became upset about the treatment of the Indian immigrants there and began to fight for their rights. Does a younger than thirteen-year-old wife have rights, I wonder but don't ask.

"Now he is fighting to get India back from the British; to give Indians their rights, their independence. Gandhi is a very popular man; has a great following of people; they even call him Mahatma—Great Soul. But he is causing a lot of unrest," Dad explains, but prophesizes that Gandhi's war will be the end for us. "With independence, it won't be long before the doors here will be closed to missionaries. The Indians want their own religion, not ours; we may have to leave." Leave? We just got here, I think. What Dad doesn't foretell is that Gandhi's war will soon come here, right to our own doorstep.

Dad writes to the Mission Board for more money to expand his school for Indian students. "We need to train teachers and preachers to carry on the work when we have to leave," he writes.

The nearsighted Mission Board replies, "No. Just keep on saving souls." But Dad doesn't listen.

I don't know much about independence, and I can't imagine India without the British. They have always just been here, everywhere really, although they generally consider themselves to be in a higher class than missionaries. They are like the Brahmins and we the outcastes, so it's not like we get together for tea or anything. What we do share with the British is a high regard for punctuality. For the Indians, though, time seems of no consequence; showing up a day or even a month late is just fine. When Dad dismisses school for the Christmas holidays, he says, "You must return on January 15; school starts then, on the 15th," and repeats it, maps it out on the calendar, and repeats it again.

"Yes, yes," the students say, wagging their heads back and forth, as Indians do instead of nodding. They smile reassuringly, "We arrive on time, yes, *Dora*, yes, most certainly." Then Dad gets red-in-the-face mad when the students arrive anywhere up to the middle of February, bright-eyed and cheerful and saying, "You are happy we return, yes?"

The British like comfort and order. They make sure policemen stand on the covered podiums in the center of busy intersections, directing traffic, and they march their troops around here and there. So we feel safe. Most importantly, the British Spencers store sells American hair curlers, permanents, chocolates, and expensive tinned spam. Then there is our travel to and from school which takes three whole days to traverse. First we ride a wide-gauge train, and then we must get off and change to a narrow gauge train because tracks, like the languages, differ from one region to another. In Madras we rent a small, cleaned to British standards, waiting room and kill time until another train takes us to Madurai, where monkeys throw coconuts at us from the roof of the train station when we try to enter to wait for the rickety bus to take us up the mountain to school.

Thanks to the British, we don't have to tote three days' worth of dry biscuits and water when we travel by train. The spick and span Spencers all along the route serve our choice of vegetarian or meat curries, tea, and drinkable water. At one station, a waiter in a starched-stiff white uniform and matching turban rushes to our window to take our order. At the next station, another delivers our order held high on a large silver tray with porcelain bowls of steaming rice, spicy curry, silver pots of tea, and gleaming utensils to go with squeaky clean china plates. The dirty dishes are whisked away at the following station.

In Madras we eat upstairs by an open-to-the-air window at a fine British restaurant—lamb, chicken, beef, or vegetarian curries, mango chutneys, anything you want. Stiff backed, ever so polite waiters say, "Yes, Madam," or "Sorry, Madam," or "Whatever you prefer, Madam." When the bold crows hop back and forth across the open window sills, greedily eyeing our food or even venturing inside to steal a bit of jewelry or a trinket carelessly left about, the self-composed, British-trained waiters rush to shoo them away. Yes, the British make traveling so pleasant—we can count on it.

Gandhi continues to walk across India, preaching nonviolence and independence. Because Mennonites are pacifists, Dad agrees with Gandhi's *Satyagrah*— gaining independence without bloodshed or violence. Will this ensure Gandhi's passage to Heaven, I wonder?

Despite Gandhi's teachings and Dad's beliefs, Muslims and Hindus battle each other, the British, and anyone else willing to fight. Roving bands of young men, the *razakars,* rush about the country, wreaking havoc as they terrorize, burn, kill, and maim, regardless of one's race, religion, or opinion on independence. Rumor has it that they are hired by the Nisam of Hyderabad to thwart the independence that will deprive His Majesty and the hundreds of other Nisams of their kingdoms.

Suddenly Gandhi's war becomes real. "There's a man in a cart; he's been shot," Mom summons Dad one day. Betty, Joanne, and I rush to the verandah to see for ourselves. In an ox cart parked under a banyan tree, sits a man, alive but hunched over, silent, motionless, with a bullet hole through his chest. We've never seen someone who has been shot, so we gaze at the large hole in the man's back, his pink inner flesh contrasting sharply with his dark skin. Flies buzz about, greedy for the small amount of blood dripping from the wound. We crouch to see the smaller hole in his chest where the bullet went in but are disappointed; he is so bent over we can barely catch a glimpse.

Dad tells Mom, "I'll have to drive him to Hyderabad City, to the hospital; but I have to finish some paperwork first."

"But Dad," Joanne and I plead on behalf of the man, who doesn't cry out, moan, or even utter a word. "Can't you go now? You have to! You do!"

"Soon," Dad promises, but I know what "soon" means when it comes to Dad. What can be more important than taking this wounded man to the hospital? Joanne and I alternate between peering at the wound and running to Dad's office to urge him to hurry. "In a moment," he says absent-mindedly, but the moment doesn't end until late in the afternoon when he finally leaves for the city, and we never hear of the poor, wounded man again.

Another day I overhear Mom and Dad's worried discussion. "The servants are upset; they say the *razakars* are here, hiding under the bridge by the station," Mom reports.

"That close, h-m-m?" The bridge to the railroad station is less than a mile away. "I'll have to go for help," and Dad rushes to the village police station to beg for protection. He returns with a small contingent of soldiers who smartly adjust their red turbans, shoulder their batons, and march in pairs around our house, placing themselves between us and the roving bands. For three days and nights, the soldiers tromp, tromp, tromp, heads held high, eyes forward. Joanne and I tiptoe from window to window to catch glimpses of them through the cracks in the long, floor-to-ceiling windows, shuttered tightly now, despite the heat. Mom doesn't sew, the Monopoly board remains untouched, Betty forgets to tell me what to do, and Dad picks up his Bible but sets it aside again as we silently wait for news that doesn't come. Each night Joanne and I lie close, and in vain urge Betty to share our bed; her bed across the room is too far away. We doze and wake to the soldiers' rhythmic marching. Round and round the brave men trudge; their tromp, tromp, tromp recedes as the soldiers round the corner of the house and then reaches a reassuring crescendo as they pass our window again.

The second night of the marching, Joanne and I scare ourselves by conjuring stories of torture and death at the hands of the *razakars*, shuddering in fear but unable to stop our wild imaginings.

"They have beards, wear dirty clothes, and will cut our throats and drink our blood," I am certain.

"No," Joanne is equally sure, "They have bright red uniforms and gold hats; they'll tear us apart, piece by piece, and feed us to the dogs."

Disgusted, Betty retreats to the living room to read by lantern light but finally joins us, only to let out a blood-curdling shriek when she pulls back her bed covers. Joanne and I burst from our bed as though shot from a cannon. Dad rushes in with his Bible in one hand and a lantern held high in the other. Surely the *razakars* have arrived, ready to murder us, but Betty points to the mouse that has made a nest under her pillow. We laugh in relief, and the mouse leaps for safety, but I notice that Mom stations herself near our door.

On the third day of the siege, Dad says, "I have to go to the train station to send a telegram. It can't wait, not one more day." He will have to pass over that bridge under which *razakars* are reported to be hiding.

"Oh, don't go," Betty, Joanne, and I plead with him, "not today, please." Mom turns aside, twisting her hands nervously, but, as a good Mennonite wife should, she says nothing.

Dad is adamant. "God's business must go on, war or not. Don't worry; God is watching over us." So the family gathers in the living room to wait. How long should this trip take? Thirty minutes? Forty-five? An hour, and then we hear the car.

"You're safe!" we cry and hug him as though he has risen from the dead. "Did you see any *razakars*? Did you send the telegram? Were there soldiers everywhere?"

He reports, "The *razakars* have left, so the soldiers are packing up. We are in God's hands now." I'd rather the soldiers stayed; I'm not sure enough about God's hands.

January comes and with it boarding school. Dad says, "You will be safer there. The war hasn't reached the hills yet."

"What about you? Why don't you come too?" Betty asks, a bold question in light of Dad's certainty that "God will protect." Yet our trunks are packed, the train is boarded, and Mom and Dad are left behind to "continue God's work" despite the danger.

At school my friends and I settle uneasily into our studies and relish every letter from home, each one a reassurance that our parents are safe. Teachers push us to study harder and exchange the lengthy hikes we normally take on weekends for skating parties in the gym and walks around the compound.

One day the principal calls my sisters, brother, and me into his office. "I've received a telegram from your father; it says that your mother is coming here; she should be here be the end of the week," and adds, "a lot of missionaries are fleeing the war."

"Does it say if Dad is coming?" Betty asks.

"It doesn't say, so I expect not," and he sends us back to class.

As we leave the office, Paul tries his hand at consolation, "You know Dad has to continue his work." I can almost hear Dad add, "God will protect." I wonder if God is considering the *razakars*.

Mom arrives and settles our family-minus-Dad into a small cottage only two miles from school. I gratefully escape the dormitory, happy to walk the two miles to school and back every day just to be with our mother. At lunch time she sends the cook to school with curry and rice packed carefully in brass containers, but she occasionally makes the lunch-run herself to be with us—or maybe just as a relief from her worries.

As the weeks go by, the progression of the war is easy to read from Mom's increasingly taut face and tight lips. Certainly Dad will join us now. Instead he writes about his trip to Bombay where he saw untended dead bodies rotting on the beaches and watched a mob turn over a bus and burn it before all the passengers could escape. This report only increases the tension in our household; studying takes a back seat to worrying. Surely Dad will get out while he can, won't he?

Without warning, he stands in the doorway in his missionary khakis, *topee* in hand, grinning as though his arrival were an everyday event. "I caught the last plane out," he says. "They took all the seats out and packed us in as tight as they could."

Joanne hugs him; Betty and Paul too. Mom beams. But I stand back, angry. Who is this man whose work comes before me, before our mother, before my sisters, my brother, and even before himself? Who is he? I don't know this man; I just don't know him. I run and hide, crying because I feel more alone now than when I cried myself to sleep all those nights in the dormitory.

CHAPTER 19

The Devil's Surprise

WHILE THE CIVIL war grinds to a halt in 1947, Mom and Dad gingerly resume their work on the mission station in Mahbubnagar. Unable to direct the war and needing something to worry him, Dad becomes obsessed with the notion that his children might stray from the straight and narrow. After all, we are surrounded day and night by heathen—the Methodist and Presbyterians, that is. I suppose that being removed from us by five hundred miles allows him to speculate on our activities at school, despite the weekly letters that we construct with care to convey the impression that we are leading Godly, Mennonite lives.

But Dad is concerned. So, with some persuasion, the Mission Board authorizes him to purchase a house across the lake from the school to serve as a dormitory for Mennonite students, which turns out to be mostly us. To fill all the beds, entry is granted to a few whose parents' religious bent is also likely to earn them a right to the narrow passage into Heaven. Unlike Boyer Hall, this dormitory sports a housefather as well as a housemother, substitute parents who will soon earn the title, Eagle Eyes.

One would suppose that all should be well in this rarified, segregated environment, but it is not.

"She's fainting," I call for Betty one evening, shortly before bed-check and lights out.

"Not again!" Betty rushes from her neighboring room.

My roommates press forward, concerned. "Should we call the housemother? Housefather?" they ask.

"No, no, no. Joanne doesn't want them to know," I protest. Then to our great relief, Joanne comes to and blinks her eyes in bewilderment.

"You aren't going to tell, are you?" she looks anxiously from one of us to another.

"No," I promise. Neither of us wants to cause trouble. Remember that time Mom threatened to call a doctor when I was delirious with fever? Who knows what might happen if it is known that Joanne is fainting every now and then.

But when the fainting spells occur three, four, and even five times a day, Betty betrays her. Joanne is shipped home immediately, and we don't see her again until Christmas break, when the car slips into the river and she almost drowns but doesn't. That is another story, although it may have some bearing on this one.

"Anemic," is the doctor's verdict. "This girl needs stronger blood. I don't have any pills or shots for this; maybe they do in America, but not here. She must drink blood squeezed from raw liver. Mix it with tomato juice; that helps a little," he tells Mother.

Hearing this, I say to my roommates, "I think her nose will become quite sore from pinching it shut to get that blood down. Sure glad it's not me!" They all agree.

Despite Joanne's dutiful compliance, she and I know that much more than anemia is causing her to lose consciousness and fall to the floor in a dead faint—more than the pink, not red enough globules that run from her veins when she is wounded. We know, but never allow to surface into actual conversation, that it is our deep, abiding fear of Eagle Eye House Father that forms the terror from which Joanne must escape. The anemia is the catalyst, but the fear that underlies it can't be cured by drinking blood, with or without tomato juice.

Our fear of Eagle Eye House Father began years ago, when we lived in California. This was a time when Joanne, Betty, Paul, and I attended a sweet, little country school. We soon developed a sense of deliciously monotonous safety because we came home every day to a mother who didn't know how to drive so never left home. But the tranquility did not last. When the Wiens brothers signed on to teach in our little school, one assigned to grades five and six, the other to seven and eight, two grades to a room, things changed.

"Great!" Mom and Dad crowed. "They are one of us; they're Mennonites, go to our church," thus bestowing on them a sort of Godliness. Dad was so pleased, probably expecting a little gospel is going to be thrown into our education for free. But it didn't turn out like that; not anything like that at all.

My first day in Alfred Wiens' class, he announced, "Boys, we're going to start you off right. I'm taking you all to the shop to cut paddles, your own paddles. Just in case you think of ever disobeying me." They returned shortly, each boy carrying a paddle resembling a sieve.

"These holes are really going to sting," Mr. Wiens explained with a grin. "You're going to yell like blazes when I use this on your backside," he said as he slapped a hole-drilled paddle against his palm. The class was silent, a hush that would become our trademark.

"Here," Mr. Wiens said, pointing to nails arrayed across the front of the room, "hang them here." Above each nail was a boy's name. Guilty, guilty, guilty, the paddles screamed. "You won't need to be reminded of the rules, now will you?" he added as the boys came forward. I wondered what he had in mind for the girls, so silence seemed the wisest course.

The paddles didn't just hang there. About once a week some Unfortunate Boy felt their sting. The thwack, thwack, thwack, and yelps held the class hostage until the culprit sniffled his way back to his seat. Occasionally the sieved wood broke on impact, and the Unfortunate Boy spent recess time carving and drilling a new one.

"You're lucky," I said to Joanne after one broken-paddle day. "If you were a year older, you'd be in my class. You'd be as scared as I am."

"I don't want to know," Joanne responded, ducking her head as though to fend off a blow. Betty was in Harold Wiens' class, so between us, we provided Joanne with daily accounts of what the Wiens brothers inflicted on students, an effort that only increased Joanne's fears.

One might expect that three frightened sisters would rush home and report on this unpleasant state of affairs, a God-given opportunity to turn our parents against our tormentors. But we never considered this, possibly because the gulf between us and our parents was too wide. Or was it because any event at school might be construed as some sort of wickedness on our part, resulting in dire consequences for us instead of the teachers? Or were we silent because we didn't want our worst fears confirmed—that our parents wouldn't care?

Whatever the reason, my sisters and I kept silent, even when classmate Willie's problems escalated. No matter how many times he was spanked, no matter how many new hole-drilled paddles he fashioned, Willie continued to have problems.

"I am a donkey," Mr. Alfred Wiens wrote on the blackboard in large, white letters that shouted louder than any animal could bray. Placing an X in the center of a large circle beneath the words, Mr. Wiens commanded, "Stand here, Willie, put your nose right on that X. Don't move until I say so."

Willie wasn't as bright as some of the rest of us. He struggled quietly with his lessons, never asked for help, and worked as hard as he could, although that usually wasn't enough for passing grades.

"How long do you think he'll make Willie stand there?" a friend whispered to me as we filed out for morning recess.

"I don't know," I answered, "Can't be all day." But I was wrong. Bewildered by all this punishment, Willie obediently stood at the chalk board while we did our lessons, went for lunch, and even afternoon recess.

"You should do something, Gwennie. You are supposed to do something," the Sunday morning, Sunday evening, and middle of the week booster lest-you-slide sermons screamed in my head. Instead, I hunched over my desk, a coward striving for invisibility. Occasionally I looked at the wide expanse of blackboard that spanned two sides of the room, plenty of space for every girl in the room to stand with her nose in a circle, plenty of room for me.

"How many hours do you think I could stand upright? What if I needed to go to the bathroom?" I asked my sisters on our way home.

"I couldn't do it," Joanne was growing more and more afraid. Being one step removed kept her on the sidelines, waiting for her turn in these brothers' classrooms—a whole year to save up her terror. "I'm not going to go to school next year. I can't be in Mr. Wiens' class." She was adamant, "I can't."

At home though, the three of us continued to remain silent. Without discussion but with clear agreement, we did not tell our parents about the paddles or about Willie.

Mr. Harold Wiens, Alfred's brother, was not only Betty's teacher but the principal to boot. We learned quickly that they were brothers, all right.

One very black day, Betty reported that Roxy, the Badest Boy of the school, angered Harold Wiens.

"You know Roxy," Betty said later, "Probably did it on purpose. But it was awful. Mr. Wiens actually growled when he lifted Roxy off the floor; flung him against the wall. What an awful sound. Roxy just lay there, didn't say a thing; was out cold. When he came to, he didn't even know what happened; just went to his seat."

Roxy never seemed quite right after that. His classmates watched him closely, measured every action, and debated endlessly whether or not he had suffered permanent damage.

Then, when everything simply couldn't get worse, it did. One evening our family was seated around the dinner table having an ordinary conversation when Dad dropped the bombshell.

"God has Called us again," he announced piously, although the phone didn't ring or a voice boom from the sky. "We are returning to India."

"Back to India? To boarding school? Oh, no," I cried. Naturally,

Joanne wasn't nearly as upset as I was. After all, God was sparing her from the Wiens brothers.

"Yes, and I have a surprise for you," Dad said. I didn't think there was any sort of surprise that could alleviate the pain of going to boarding school, far away from home and far from Mom and Dad. Yet Dad was so pleased with himself that he was just about bursting. "Your mother and I are concerned about you there at boarding school, especially being among people who aren't One Of Us," meaning the Presbyterians and Methodists. "We want the best for you, especially for your spiritual welfare. We don't like to worry so much about you up there in the hills." I was happy to hear that they were going to worry about us, not totally forgotten as I often feared. Knowing Dad, though, I suspected that he was about to give us each a new Bible or something.

"So," he continued with the air of a parent about to present his children with an unexpected Christmas gift right in the middle May, "I have persuaded Miss Ruth, your piano teacher, to come along with us when we go." Well, that was fine then. Miss Ruth was really nice and made actual recordings of the best performer's memorized piece at monthly recitals. Betty, of course, had lots of those little black disks stashed away already.

But Dad wasn't finished. "I have persuaded Harold Wiens to go along too; and his family, of course. They'll arrive in a year or so when they get their papers in order." Dad beamed and looked around, expecting whoops and hollers of joy and all sorts of, "Thanks, Dad. We'll be happy to go back to boarding school now."

But Betty, Joanne, and I just stared at him in disbelief. How could he? How could he have done this to us? But what could we say? Or do? Nothing. It was too late; far, far too late.

Many months later, after we went home again for the holidays and returned, Joanne has downed pounds of raw liver and gallons of blood and gained enough strength to come back to school. Her spirit has miraculously gained strength as well. I know this for certain because she does not faint when Mr. Eagle Eye Housefather—Harold Wiens—watches his son swing a cat around and around by its tail in the front yard. Mr. Eagle Eye cackles in amusement without a word of rebuke. Joanne, though, doesn't even turn pale. Instead, to my utter astonishment, Joanne marches right up to Mr. Eagle Eye, looks straight into his eyes, and proclaims loudly, "That's cruel! You should stop him!"

My, oh my; taking this sort of risk takes an awful lot of guts. Who knows whether any minute she will be slung against a wall like Roxy or be required to stick her nose against the nearest tree, like Willie? I can see right then and there that something has certainly changed, Joanne facing up to him like this. Then, before Mr. Eagle Eye can recover from the shock, Joanne turns around and marches away, head held high.

Now, I can't tell you if it was drinking all that raw liver blood in tomato juice that did it or sinking to the bottom of a muddy river and coming back up alive (you'll hear about that yet), but I do know one thing—I am awfully proud of my sister Joanne!

CHAPTER 20

The Born Again Car

BACK IN CALIFORNIA, before this term in India even began, the folks in one Mennonite Church dug deeply into their pockets and brought forth enough of their hard-earned cash to provide our family with a new car. This was accomplished when Reverend Friesen held the congregation captive at the close of the service one Sunday morning. Despite an occasional tug-of-war between the zealous preacher and an unwilling giver, the promise of Heavenly rewards usually won out.

"I pledge three hundred dollars," one hand went up; then another, "Four hundred." Nudged by his wife, Mr. Schmidt reluctantly raised his hand, "Five hundred."

"I know you had a good crop of grapes this year," the Reverend swiftly admonished from the pulpit, eyeing several reluctant farmers. "I need a whole train-car of raisins from each of you."

Shame-faced, Mr. Schmidt waggled his fingers just high enough to be seen above his short-cropped hair, pledging some of the proceeds from his precious crops for which he had had other plans. In thirty minutes the California farmers pledged enough to buy a spanking new, black car for our family. That was how it came about that we returned to the mission field with a three-seater, black station wagon, and the congregation of the California Mennonite Church was a giant step closer to Heaven.

On the day that the New Car was ceremonially blessed, the congregation sang praises to God and then spilled into the church basement for a pot-luck celebration. At that moment, who could have guessed that this car would someday sink to watery depths, become a tomb, and rise again?

While Joanne and I took every chance to suck in the smell of the new leather and fuss over rights to window seats, Dad and Paul quickly built a wooden rack on top of the New Car for the mountains of luggage that accompanies our every journey. The New Car was ready to make the trip to Minnesota for The Preparation Period, return to San Francisco, and then sit quietly in the hold of a ship during the long voyage to China and Singapore, through oceans, and on to India.

While our family said tearful goodbyes to friends and a few relatives who journeyed all the way to San Francisco to see us off, Dad ran up and down the dock, futilely shouting orders.

"Don't let those crates bump up against my car! Watch those barrels; they're going to put a dent in that car!" He finally grew silent when the New Car was wrapped in a large net, lifted by crane, and deposited in the bowels of the *S. S. Marine Swallow*, our temporary home.

We were off! During the next four weeks, my sisters, brother, and I dashed about the ship, played games, and intently watched the Catholic priests who were journeying to their various missions. All the while, the New Car slumbered in the hold. With no souls to save, Dad indulged himself in worry. He slipped down into the dark, dank chamber to check. Every single day his report was the same, "The New Car is doing just fine." God was with us and our precious car, for sure. Of course He was! Most of southern California and some folks in Minnesota were on their knees, praying for us.

Life generally moves slowly at a mission station on the hot Indian plains, but things certainly pick up when my parents' arrive, especially with the New Car in tow. People materialize out of nowhere. Some travel long distances on the rutted roads by ox cart, many trudge the paths by foot, and children ride their parents' backs or, bundled in rags, are perched on their mothers' hips—all to catch a glimpse of a car so new its tires sport no patches, its paint is still shiny, and the side-view mirrors are so clear that the women push and shove to catch a glimpse of their own images. First exclaiming, they then giggle shyly and cover their mouths with the tag end of their *saris*. Everyone agrees; this station wagon is truly a thing of beauty and certainly God-sent. Would they think the same if they knew that one day this car is destined to bring great sorrow to our doorstep?

As soon as my parents arrive at the mission station, Dad erects a special shed to house the New Car and purchases a padlock to keep it safe. After that, the rituals surrounding the car are established. Petrol being scarce, Dad infrequently announces that he is going to "get the car out." With that, folks from the entire compound rush to gaze at and join in on the action, annoying Dad with their chattering and unsolicited advice. Dad always arms five or six school-boys with large sticks and directs them to chase out the rats nesting in the car. That done, he backs out, very, very slowly. Women chatter nervously and clutch their children who wrench free and dare one another to touch the moving vehicle. Young boys rush forward to brush away the dust that has turned the black car brown. Everything ready, Dad announces where he is going—to the train station; to Hyderabad City, 40 miles and 4 hours away; to another mission station; or just for a drive to keep the car in running order.

This sets off a new hullabaloo. "I need to visit a friend who lives near the train station," or "My mother is dying and lives near the city," or "I need to see the doctor at Shamshabad." Everyone wants a ride. Reluctantly, Dad packs ten or even twelve souls into the car and allows six or eight to stand on the running boards. Meanwhile, several young boys perch on the back bumper, grinning triumphantly at their friends. The car zooms down the drive, but rounding a curve, the bumper-travelers fall off and run home, laughing and boasting of their daring.

Dad mutters, "I need to make a rule against taking people along." And the car bounces past the gates and out of the compound, traveling at a speedy ten-miles-an-hour, down the dusty road.

Driving in India is like having one's personal roller coaster. Where there are roads, the surface resembles Grandma's washboard; where there aren't, the car bumps along the narrow furrows chiseled by ox carts. In some places there are no roads or furrows, so Dad simply forges his own path. But the last five miles into Hyderabad City are paved, so when my sisters, brother, and I happen to be home for the holidays and accompany Dad on trips to the city, we eagerly watch the speedometer—ten, then twenty miles an hour! The wind blasts our faces as we hang our heads out the windows, whizzing past ox carts, camels, and even an occasional elephant. The natives stop to watch, open-mouthed; I feel just a bit superior, then guilty for it.

Bridges are rare, so getting the car stuck crossing a shallow river or stream is almost guaranteed. Dad isn't worried.

He says, "We'll wait for an ox cart to come along; sure to be one any moment now." Sure enough, one does, and Dad hitches the owner's oxen to the front bumper, urges the animals forward, and when the car is free, he pays the owner for the loan of his precious property.

Meanwhile, we are allowed to wade in the water as long as we watch out for snakes and scorpions. Wading is also permitted when a tire goes flat. We search out a stream where Dad can submerge the inner tube, find where air fizzles out, and patch it.

Driving at night in India provides its own sensations. Lonely travelers, we have just our headlights to keep us company and guide the way. Only twinkling pinpoints of light from oil lamps in distant villages suggest we are not entirely alone.

On one such occasion, the sense of eerie mystery of night travel became real when Dad abruptly stopped the car.

"Look," Dad whispered. A tiger, caught in the beam of our headlights, momentarily stopped to look our way. Unperturbed, he then glided majestically across the road he now owned.

"Oh-h-h," we sighed at the magnificence of this king whose powerful muscles rippled with his every step. Yet, we were also relieved at being safely ensconced within the metal shell of our faithful car.

No matter when we travel at night, the bouncing car lulls me to sleep, and Dad lovingly carries me to bed when we get home. These are the best times.

The Old Car

A MISSIONARY'S CAR is important to the saving of souls. Before the gift of the new car from the California Mennonites, Dad nursed our Old Car through thick and thin. This car was tired, having begun its service to God long before I was born. So faded by the tropical sun, it no longer could be called The Blue Car or the Green Car. Anyway, nobody remembered anymore what color it originally was. Yet Dad could resurrect the Old Car if necessary.

When Joanne and I were too young for boarding school, Dad occasionally announced, "Time to go touring," and tinkered with the Old Car until it was ready for service.

"Can we go? Can we?" Joanne and I would plead.

"Take the girls, I need a rest," Mother would say, clearly willing to have us out from underfoot for a few days. "Taking the trailer?" The answer would tell her how long we'd be gone.

Dad and a carpenter had built a small house on wheels. For touring, it was attached behind the car and bumped along, forward or sideways, depending on how well worn the ruts were. Shallow, wide, and smooth were best. With the trailer in tow, Dad comfortably traveled from village to village, preaching the gospel and saving souls. The trailer had bunks and even a tiny shower stall. When Joanne and I were invited along, we squeezed into the stall and poured water over ourselves to wash off the dust. Evenings, the cook squatted in the dirt, arranged a few large stones in a circle around a small fire, plopped a pan on top, and came forth with a curry fit for a king. Dad lit the Coleman lantern, hung it high, and waited. The beam attracted crowds and bugs, alike. Dad's voice rose and fell with passion, sorrow, or pleading. The people were mesmerized by this strange, white man and his words, but Joanne and I fell asleep, comforted by his preaching, which assured us that he was near.

Cars are essential to missionary life for a number of reasons. Again, long ago, before Joanne and I went to school, there was the time when our old, beaten-by-cruel-roads Old Car was put to use beyond the saving of souls. This was when my sisters and brother needed to be brought home from boarding school for the Christmas break.

Uncle John Wiebe, whose children also needed to return home, came up with a plan.

"Why not fetch them by car? The school is only five hundred miles away. Besides, driving saves train fare."

Dad agreed. "We'll have to take out the seats, though, to make room," Dad said. "On the way back, if we squeeze you, Aunty Wiebe, Anna, and me into the front seat, we can fit the twelve children in the back. But we'll have to take out the seats; won't be room otherwise."

That return trip lasted two long weeks. All shoes and *topees* were stuffed into pillow cases and tied to the back bumper. Luggage was secured to the roof of the car, and the two biggest boys, Paul and John, joyfully perched themselves over the headlights. They took delight in shouting warnings of potholes, slow moving ox carts, or other impediments ahead. That left the rest of us children to sit in two rows, backs to the windows, facing each other, our entwined feet braided down the middle.

Packed in tighter than seeds in a papaya, we alternately whined, cried, or fought until Uncle John began to tell an endless stream of stories. "Tell it again," we cried when he told the story of the boy who was chased through a graveyard one dark night, only to discover that it was his own corduroy pants that swished with the movement of his legs and sounded ever so much like footsteps.

At night the men threw a tarp on the ground for our weary bodies; we fell asleep, too exhausted and sore to fear for snakes, scorpions, lions, or tigers. "Don't worry," Uncle John and Dad said in unison. "God is with us," as was our faithful Old Car.

The New Car

NOW WE HAVE the New Car, courtesy of the California Mennonites. It serves us as faithfully as that Old Car did; so well, indeed, that we begin to take it for granted. But not for long. Everything is about to change in one single, disastrous moment.

Joanne is still at home, drinking blood and eating raw liver to heal her anemia, but this ordeal is offset by the pleasure she receives from playing with our new baby sister, Lois. Paul, Betty, Margaret, and I are ready to come home for vacation, and Mom plans to fetch us. Upon hearing this, the Klassen family decides to accompany Mom and my sisters.

"A great chance to take a break from the heat," the Klassens say.

"Take the New Car," Dad offers generously. "I'd like to go, but I'm having difficulty with the school. Go ahead, take the car; I won't need it."

Missionary Klassen gratefully accepts, so he, his wife, their two young sons, my sisters Joanne and baby Lois, and Mom start out on the journey together.

Meanwhile, Paul, Betty, Margaret, and I have long since packed our army-surplus footlockers, impatient to be home. Long before Mom and the Klassens are due, we wait for the crunch of the wheels and the honk of a horn, eager to cheer our release from school. Instead, our housemother brings us a telegram.

"Somebody is dead, drowned," she says. "They won't be coming. You're to take the bus down the *ghat* and catch the overnight train to Madras."

"Is it Mom? Joanne? The baby?" We must know.

"I don't think so; it only says something about the Klassens," she says and gets us on our way.

That night, huddled together in a small train compartment, even the click, click, click of the train's wheels on the track fails to bring the expected relief that sleep can bring. Instead, each of us huddles in our own silence, gazing out the windows at a landscape as dark as our terror. We know that voicing our thoughts will make the fear uncontainable and restraining it would be like trying to put a genie back in a bottle. As the rising sun finally dispels the dark, we arrive in Madras, our destination and our hope. Anxious that the train might resume its journey before our luggage is unloaded, we hastily drag out our trunks and scan the crowded platform for Dad. People scramble to either disembark or board the train, others rush to greet friends, and vendors weave in and out of the crowd, screaming their wares. People are everywhere. But no Dad in sight.

"Dad? Where's Dad?" I ask anxiously. "The telegram; it said he would meet us."

"Don't worry, he'll be here; he will." Paul is certain.

Always practical, Betty asks, "How much money do we have?" Searching, we come up with only a few *rupees* she saved from her allowance.

"That's not even enough for breakfast," I whine, translating the knot in my stomach into manageable hunger pangs. Margaret, only six-years-old, begins to cry. But no decision is necessary as Dad rushes up, a life boat to our drowning.

"Mom? Lois? Joanne?" we ask urgently.

"They are fine, just fine," Dad's eyes fill with tears. "It's Auntie Klassen and Justin; they drowned, down in the river." We stare. "Right now we have to rush to catch another train. We're going to a Lutheran mission station in Radhala, where Mother and the others are waiting." Then he relates the details of the past few days.

It seems that when Mom, Joanne, Lois, and the missionary Klassen family were on their way to escort us home, they had to cross the deep, bridgeless Krishna River. They paid the fee for a barge to carry the New Car across the river. For the short ride, Mom maintained her spot in the middle seat, clutching six-month-old baby Lois. Joanne remained scrunched between pieces of luggage in the back. The Klassen family climbed out and stood on deck to enjoy a brief reprieve from the stifling, sun-heated air inside the car. Then the barge was firmly secured by rope to a large ferry boat, all to the entertainment of the ferry's passengers who lined the rails to watch. As the ferry and its now Siamese twin, the barge, were about to shove off, a heavy lorry rolled up. At this moment, the deadly decision was made to allow the lorry to drive aboard, right behind our car. The ferry and its piggy-backed barge then floated safely across the river, but about thirty yards from the far shore, two unrelated but significant events took place. Mrs. Klassen and Justin began to reenter the car, and the captain gave the order to untie the barge in preparation for landing, thinking the barge's momentum would allow it to slip right into the dock. However, upon loading the lorry, no concern had been given to balancing the two vehicles. Consequently, untethered from the ferry, the barge tipped. The car, the lorry, and both families plunged twenty feet down to the bottom of the murky river.

Mother instinctively grasped six-month-old baby Lois by her little arms. Seeing the dim light of an open window, she thrust the baby forward and threaded her way out and up. They gasped for air upon reaching the surface, but Mother didn't know how to swim. As Dad would later remind us many times, God sent a small fishing boat to just that spot at just that moment. The fishermen quickly grasped Mother and Lois and pulled them into their boat. Meanwhile, twelve-year-old Joanne escaped through a back window, floated up, and swam for some distance before she, too, was rescued by kindly fishermen. Mr. Klassen and Jimmie, who had been standing beside the car, swam to shore. But for Mrs. Klassen and Justin, caught by the door as they were reentering the car, the vehicle became a tomb.

A crowd gathered immediately, but the Telegu of our missions was not the language of this area. Nonetheless, with much gesturing and shouting, a deaf mute, skilled in diving, was fetched to bring up the bodies. Meanwhile, the crowd conveyed the welcomed news that there was a mission station only a few miles down the road. By ox cart, the survivors and the bodies were taken there and compassionate Lutheran missionaries took charge. Within hours, the bodies were buried and Dad telegrammed to complete the mission of fetching us from school. Then the survivors settled in to cope with their grief and wait for Dad to gather us from school, return, and drive us all back home in a borrowed car.

"You're alive!" my sisters, brother, and I cry, as we enter the Lutheran mission compound and see Mom, baby Lois, and Joanne unharmed. We hug, weep, and hug again. Before we can hear all the details of their horror, an increasingly loud rumbling turns our attention to the New Car. Now resurrected from the deep, it is being towed into the compound. Seeping water from every crevice and cavity, the poor vehicle is deposited, left to lie on its side—beaten, dented, and smeared—inside and out—with river-bottom mud. Like the bodies that had quickly reeked of death, so does the upholstery already emit the stench of decay. Must we bury this dear friend as well?

"No," says Dad, reading my thoughts. "We'll ship it to Madras. Maybe it can be repaired; I think it just might." So we thank the Lutherans, make a last visit to the graves that are so far from home that we will never again visit them, and limp home.

Two months later, my sisters, brother and I prepare for the long journey back to school.

"I'm going to take you this time," Dad says. "I want to stop in Madras and check on the New Car." And we do. Stepping into the repair shop, we look about expectantly.

"Here," says the chief mechanic, smiling enthusiastically, "here it is." But it isn't. The engine is in pieces on the floor. Beside it are springs, the skeletal remains of the seats, and some large pieces of metal that resemble the hood, fenders, and doors.

"Yes," insists the mechanic, wagging his head vigorously. "It will be just fine. It will be done in six months' time, for certain. Good as new, ver-r-ry, ver-r-ry good," he promises, shaking hands with each of us in turn. We sigh, smile politely, and leave.

Yet, sure enough, six months later our beloved New Car, now born-again, is ready for the adventures ahead, and, for all I know, it will bounce along the rutted roads of the Indian plains for a hundred years to come.

CHAPTER 21
The Ladies

- *Reflection by my older sister Betty*

Dear Reader,

To understand an account of the unique comings and goings of the single women who reside on every Mennonite mission station, some explanation is in order. Upon my sister Gwen's request, I provide here an introduction to the ladies who dedicate their lives to teaching young children and caring for the multitudes who seek care for illnesses for which they themselves are unable to find relief. These women have an impact on our lives, although only mininmally.

Sincerely,
Elizabeth (Betty) Hiebert

EVERY MISSION COMPOUND has two large, whitewashed bungalows, one two-storied with verandahs all around, upstairs and down, for the missionary-in-residence and his family. The smaller bungalow is one-storied, built just large enough to fit two single ladies who have given up on any chance of marriage and turned their lives over to teaching and healing in this far off land, overflowing with those who desperately and eagerly need their services. Thus, back in America, they are not viewed as spinsters but with awe as women who sacrifice their lives for Christ. The Ladies, we call them.

The Indians' among whom we live view these women quite differently. To them, the missionary himself is addressed as *dora*—a term that denotes a rich, powerful man, someone to be subservient to and treat with utmost respect as he has much to-which-you- might-lay-your-hands-upon. Not completely understanding the meaning of the word *dora,* some missionaries demand that they be so addressed, thinking that *dora* will substitute for "Mr." or "Sir." For example, not "Mr. Hiebert" but *"Dora* Hiebert" or even simply *"Dora."*

However, according to traditional and sometimes mysterious Indian customs, many Indian *doras* have a first wife, his major wife. He also has a second and even a third wife who are called *dorasanis.* Therefore, it is not surprising to them that the white man resides with his first wife in the large bungalow and then, as he should, keeps his second and third wives in a smaller, second house. Thus, for the missionary to be ensconced in the large bungalow with his wife and family is proper, as are the ladies, the *dorasanis,* in the second, less impressive bungalow.

When my father makes the trek to Hyderabad City, hours away and over rough, washboard roads, Mother occasionally begs off because she is too tired, too pregnant, or has had too much of his company. At such times, Father invites The Ladies to share the ride as the Mission Board does not deem ladies fit to be in possession of their own cars. According to God's law, the male is the head of the household and in this case, the compound. At any rate, The Ladies must either take the bus, train, or wait patiently for the missionary's invitation to ride along to the city to complete their shopping.

According to Indian custom, Mother and The Ladies are acting appropriately. Indian values dictate that the first wife should stay home and remain modestly unseen. The second and third wives are the ones the man can squire about in public, enjoying their company openly and at his leisure. Many years of study are required before missionaries learn the ins and outs of Indian customs and, even if they do, their Mennonite upbringing and Western mores usually dictate their behavior. Consequently, when the missionary goes to the city with one or two of The Ladies, he throws a child or two in the back seat, righteous in his unwillingness to be alone in the company of a woman other than his own wife. The Indians and the missionary, Ladies in tow, wave at each other as the car leaves the compound, each smiling about the properness of it all.

In addition to the traditional whitewashed bungalows, squeezed within our Mahbubnager mission compound are a church, servants' quarters, a deep well, and gardens. Boarding quarters for students were added as this station boasts the only coeducational high school in the entire region. As is every other important building in the country, ours is surrounded by whitewashed walls that come together at the front gate which is guarded by a withered, little, old man who takes pride and much joy over his power to open the gates, or not. His hut is built so that he can tend the entrance day and night, thus keeping the missionaries and ladies free of loitering cattle, chickens, beggars, and those with leprosy, elephantitis, or other equally horrific diseases. If turned away by our gatekeeper, some gain entry by wailing so loudly and so long that Dad relents and gestures to allow them in. Woe to the traveler who comes at night because the gatekeeper must first be wakened and then persuaded to open the gates, which he does with considerable grumbling, expecting *baksheesh* for his efforts.

Some mission stations have a building just for educating young children, others do not. When no roof or walls are provided, The Lady who teaches must conduct classes under the tree that provides the most shade. All stations have a small building for the other unmarried lady, a nurse. There she tends the sick that come in droves, day and night, seeking to have a boil lanced, a broken bone set, or a cure for worms and other such ailments. Once tended, they disappear as mysteriously as they came. The seriously ill must remain for days or even weeks, so they arrive with family members who set up camp under a nearby tree to cook for and tend to the ailing relative, services not provided by the mission.

The Shamshabad mission station is unique, having not only a hospital but a full-fledged doctor, Dr. Shellenburg, who is also one of The Ladies. By custom, Indian men are reluctant to allow their wives to be treated by a male doctor as treatment might involve exposing a wife's private territory to a man other than the husband. With a female doctor available, men graciously allow their wives to make use of her services. These women are grateful that their babies now have a better than the usual one-third chance of survival. They are also highly appreciative of the relief that is forthcoming for female ailments that, until now, the women simply endured if a home remedy or prayer did not render aid. If a missionary's wife is about to give birth, Dr. Shellenburg schedules her arrival at that mission station a week or two before the due date.

American and Canadian ladies willingly, or out of despair of finding a husband, arrive regularly in India—Miss Nichols, Miss Schmidt, Miss Lorenz, Miss Wiens, Miss Pankratz, Miss this and Miss that. They are always here, busy with their duties, interfering minimally with the *dora's* comings and goings. The Ladies are pleasant company on the verandah in the cool of the evening, just before the lamps are lit. They are even polite recipients of the *dora's* advice, sought or not. In our case, we and The Ladies live fairly separate lives—they in their Ladies Bungalow and we in ours. I expect they will live there and die there, and mostly they do. But one does escape. This story I leave to Gwen to tell.

Back on that straight-from-hell day, when Mrs. Klassen and Justin drowned in the river, but Mother, Joanne, and Lois were saved, the ripple effect was far and wide, even reaching one of the sacrificing-herlifeforChrist Ladies. After the accident, Dad gathered my sisters, brother, and me from boarding school and together with what was left of the Klassen family, drove the dusty, dirt roads back to our mission station.

Mom sat beside Dad in the front seat, tightly holding baby Lois as though the threat of a watery grave was always imminent. Betty, Joanne, and I were squished beside Mr. Klassen, in the back. Jimmie, his remaining son, turned himself into a ball of misery at our feet. The days of travel were broken when we stopped to sleep at rest houses, government-built bungalows placed here and there for weary travelers. It was a long, long trip.

Bored, my eyes wandered to poor Mr. Klassen. He sat hour after hour with his head lowered into his hands, tears occasionally spilling down over his son. But I, being a teenager, began to think that maybe Mr. Klassen will soon need a new wife, someone to care.for him, to console him in his grief.

"I, I could do that," I whispered to myself. So, in the long silent hours of riding over bumpy, dusty roads toward home, I began to fantasize about what a wonderful wife I would make for poor Mr. Klassen. I envisioned wiping his tears, putting his head on my shoulder, and enclosing his large, old—at least 40—body in my arms. Such thoughts served to while away the many hours during those long days. Before I fell asleep each night, I luxuriated in the fantasy of the gift of myself that I could offer to poor Mr. Klassen.

It seemed, though, that I was not alone in these thoughts. On one of our infrequent stops, Betty accosted me.

"You, and Joanne too," she hissed, "you think you are going to marry Mr. Klassen, don't you!"

Surprised that she was able to read my thoughts, I denied any such thing. "That's just plain stupid. You must be thinking of that for yourself. Otherwise, you wouldn't have thought of it," I threw it right back at her. But I began to watch her and Joanne for signs of their willingness to provide for Mr. Klassen. Which of us would he choose, if he were to choose?

"Me," I said to myself, "I am the best, the prettiest." Of this I was certain.

When we finally reached the Nagarkurnool mission station, we were compelled to say goodbye to Mr. Klassen and Jimmie, leave them to their grief and loneliness, and continue home. Soon caught up with Christmas and the lazy life of living in the plains, my thoughts of Mr. Klassen soon dwindled into dust.

A year later, Mr. Klassen had been easily replaced by several knights. At school, I loved, fell out of love, and loved again. Then a letter arrived from Mother and my attention returned to poor Mr. Klassen. I savored these tidbits from my parents that arrived every week or two, letters that my sisters, brother, and I shared. When my turn came to read one particular letter, I found a spot on a grassy hill and sat down to read.

Dear Paul, Betty, Gwen, Joanne and Margaret,

Things are much the same here at the mission station. Aaron burned his leg when he tried to cook borscht; the cattle got into the vegetables, so Gardener John is upset. Dad has been touring for the past week and should be home tomorrow. The real excitement is Mr. Klassen's marriage to Miss Pankratz. Already we hear she is carrying twins. We look forward to seeing you back home for vacation soon.

Love, Mom

I let the letter flutter to the grass. Well, I thought. He didn't wait for me, did he? But Miss Pankratz! What happened to sacrificingher-lifeforChrist? There she was all the time, in the Ladies' Bungalow, right next to his big house. The Indians had it right, after all. Mr. Klassen did have his *dorisani.*

CHAPTER 22
The Devil Made Us Do It

"WE CAN HANDLE this one, can't we? Should be a piece of cake!" says John, the Tom Sawyer of my eighth grade class in boarding school. He leads us, but not always down the path of righteousness. We have whizzed through Miss Little's sixth grade and gained in numbers in the seventh—twenty-two, the largest class in boarding school. Yet, like the moss growing on the trees in the surrounding forests, we are gathering a tarnished reputation.

"Of course we can," is the class's enthusiastic response to John's challenge. We are off and running with our plan to defeat even the most ardent of teachers.

While some teachers might say that we, the students, are culpable for what happens this term, Miss Slifert is really to blame. Weren't we just fine under her tutelage? We studiously slaved away at grammar, science, history, and math as good missionary children should. But then her contract was up and she left, taking our good behavior with her.

"This is Mrs. Cawthorne," Papa Phelps, the principal, arrives to introduce Miss Slifert's replacement. "She has volunteered to finish out the year. I expect you to be courteous and show her what good students you are." He waits a few moments, we beam angelically, and Papa says to Mrs. Cawthorne, "Let me know if you need anything." With that, he leaves her to her fate.

Mrs. Cawthorne is a tall, slender lady. And old, at least thirty-five. Her plain, unfashionable dress just meets the brown socks that are neatly folded down around her ankles, just above her sturdy brown shoes.

She starts right in with a speech obviously prepared to get her through the first moments with us, "I'm so glad to be here. I'm anxious to get started, to get to know each of you. Miss Slifert left a note about what wonderful students you are."

We sit quietly, and like a lion eyeing his prey, we watch her every movement. She smiles, hesitates, and coughs nervously. John smiles devilishly, our cue that Mrs. Cawthorne is going to be a pushover.

Within a week, John says, "Cawthy is bo-o-ring." He pushes his round, dirty glasses back up the bridge of his nose, takes his gum from behind his ear, and pops it into his mouth. He glances around our class which has gathered around the flag pole after tea.

"Can't stand her," I agree. "What're we going to do about it?"

"Maybe we should give her a chance," Margie chimes in. Margie doesn't have a mean bone in her body and can even be trusted with one's darkest secrets. Some persuasion will be required to get her in line with what is brewing.

Joan suggests we start with a simple experiment. "Let's see if she'll let us knit in class." Knitting is the latest fad among the girls. We knit without criticism before breakfast, between tea and supper, and a bit before lights out. But knitting in class is something no student would think of asking for. Granting or not granting this permit will be Cawthy's first test. Winner take all.

"Mrs. Cawthorne, do you mind if we knit in class?" We have persuaded Nell to pop the question. Nell is tall and confident, the most commanding figure among us, most likely to be taken seriously.

"Hm-m, ah-h," Mrs. Cawthorne is clearly sitting on the fence here.

"Miss Slifert always let us," I lie, crossing my fingers behind my back.

"She did," some of the girls chime in, nodding in agreement.

Cawthy continues to hem and haw but can't seem to find an objection. "BecauseIsaidso," is seemingly not in her vocabulary, a fact of which we gleefully take note.

We win. For the next few weeks, we girls create sweaters, caps, and shawls during Cawthy's lectures. The notch carved in the front of the desk drawers by innocent-looking but rebellious boys allows us to stow the yarn in the drawers, drawing the thread out as needed. So there we sit, knitting away, listening but not listening to Cawthy's honey-sweet, yet hesitant voice, not at all like Miss Slifert's solid-as-a-rock, I'm-in-charge tone.

Despite the knitting and the half listening, the remainder of our brains requires a new challenge, a next step in our plan. Margie, now on board, Nell, Joan, and I buddy up.

"Joan, you're good at English," I say. "I can work on history; my Dad really pushes history at home; all the time."

"Yeh, and Margie, you love science," Nell catches on quickly. "I'll do the math."

For three weeks each completes the work for her assigned subject, and the other three copy it. Thus, we expend one-fourth the usual effort on our studies and have energy left over for other interests. Answers to test questions are passed around via small pieces of paper pre-stuffed into our pockets. We take immense pride in our success. John would have been proud had he known, but given that knowledge, he would have demanded a piece of the action.

Too soon, Cawthy begins to increase the amount of time she stands near our desks, watching us four sinners more and more carefully.

"Guess we'll have to stop," Margie concludes. We reluctantly agree.

The cheating game is over, but the punishment for our sins should be slight, easily forgiven by God. Should make just a dent in our Heaven's credit account. We certainly have money in the bank by now. We have faithfully said nightly onyourknees prayers for thirteen years—365 X 13— plus three times a day at meals. We could even add our parents' daily prayers for our well being. Maybe even thrice daily for some of us who teeter on the brink.

But most of our Heavenly credit is destroyed in a flash when our class, in a moment of boredom, or creativity, succumbs to temptation.

John's mind has been devilishly busy. Gathering the class at the flagpole again, he says, "If Miss Slifert can be shipped off to America, so can Cawthy. We can handle this, piece of cake."

"Brilliant," the class is in agreement. Cawthy just isn't like Miss Slifert.

"We can't bring Miss Slifert back, but we shouldn't have to put up with Cawthy, should we?" says Paul, always supportive of John.

We devise a plan. While the girls knit, gossip, and bury Mrs. Cawthorne with an endless stream of innocuous questions, the boys throw spit wads, scuffle their feet loudly, and feign innocence when desks tip over. After a few futile attempts to control this onslaught, Mrs. Cawthorne decides her health is failing. She leaves. Victorious, we no longer see teachers as ThoseWhoMustBeObeyed but as prey whose vulnerabilities we can seek out and exploit.

Papa Phelps opens the door, a new recruit in tow. "Class, this is Miss Jaisinghani, your new teacher." She is a tiny, Indian woman, soft spoken and gentle. She glides into the room like a dancer, her pastel pink *sari* shouting soft vulnerability. This time Papa lingers, watching, then reluctantly leaves.

"I don't think he trusts us," Ralph whispers to John.

"Of course he doesn't," John smiles.

Miss Jaisinghani is accustomed to British students who rise when called upon, are humble, and would rather be snake-bit than raise their voices. We are loud and prone to deceit.

"I'm James," says John. Following his lead, we see this as a God-given chance to change our names.

"We have finished with grammar. Miss Slifert let us do what we like during English period," says one confident soul.

"In America we are allowed to take tests with our books open," says another.

"Yes, and we are supposed to work together to come up with the right answers, so we can learn from each other," adds still another.

Miss Jaisinghani gives it her best for a few weeks, and leaves. We are quite delighted with our new-found power.

"We did it!" exclaims John, slapping his thigh and then ruffling his unruly hair. We do a quick jig around the flagpole. We are on a roll.

The next teacher is overwhelmed when we put a snake in Tommy's desk, cut in two so that half hangs down on one side and half protrudes out the other. Tommy's shriek is drowned by the teacher's scream and the slam of the door as she flees. Another casualty, another victory.

One, then another, gives us a try—six teachers in all. With each victim, we mark the number of days they tolerate our increasingly outrageous behavior. We are winning the contest that we ourselves invented.

As with all games, the final whistle must eventually sound. Papa Phelps marches into our class, smiling this time. Having grown smug, we fail to take note of this important clue. Instead, we don falsely angelic faces and sit with hands neatly folded.

"I have found another teacher," he says, "I think you'll like this one." We are not alarmed. We are drunkenly cocky in our knowledge that any brave soul willing to try her hand at subduing our wild and wicked ways can be persuaded otherwise within weeks, even days. Maybe hours this time.

Papa Phelps beckons to the woman waiting just outside the door. She is a large woman, tall, commanding in stature. She stomps solemnly to the front of the class. Her dress is dark and severely cut, she wears sturdy, no nonsense shoes—and she is Eddie's mother. Eddie, the boy who sits quietly at the back of the class and whose only interest is in flying paper airplanes, says not a word. In chorus, we swivel in our seats to stare. Eddie The Traitor slinks low in his seat.

"Get out your books," commands Eddie's mother, arms crossed, an evil glint in her eyes. The wind completely driven from our sails, we shrink back to normal size, get out our books, and know for certain that the game is over, the final whistle has sounded.

CHAPTER 23
Keep Your Mouth Shut

NOTHING BUT LUNCH and afternoon tea break up the long days in boarding school here in the hills. While our parents toil on the hot plains, we, their children, are abandoned to the wiles and whims of teachers and house parents who force us to study Latin, math, science, and history, English, and practice the piano—every day. Well, except for weekends. Beginning after supper and ending at bed time, we must be in study hall, dead or alive. Assigned to seats far from our best friends, we complete—or ignore—our homework.

I whine to my sister Betty, "I hate school! I hate studying! Anyway, I'll never make straight As like you and Joanne and Paul. Besides, I'm already failing geometry, so they're going to write Mom and Dad."

"Oh, no. You have to try," she says, alarmed. "I'll help you with geometry, every night. I know they'll let me during study hall."

Unconvinced, I attack, "You and Joanne always say I'm just going to marry a farmer, have twelve children, and never set foot in a college."

"We were just teasing," she says, then sends a barb of her own. "If you didn't sneak off so often and tried harder, you could make better grades."

"I go to the woods, that's all. To Bear Shola or Fairy Falls," I confess. "I'd die if I couldn't go there. I don't care if it's against the rules."

Despite Betty's efforts, I continue to suffer through hours of Mr. Musil's indecipherable Latin, Mr. Ruggerio's frog dissections, Mrs. Thomas's sentence diagrams, and Mr. Root's mysterious geometry proofs, knowing that failure is just around the next corner.

Other than sneaking off the compound, what gets me through the days are the weekends. I am in heaven when my friends and I put on our walking shoes, don our knapsacks, fill our canteens, and hike the marvelous hills surrounding us—pure paradise. When we hike, the sunlight slants down through the dense trees, trying to reach the floor below. We inhale the sweet smell of eucalyptus and pine, joyful to be away from school, joyful just to be here. We tread the lush carpets of grass as we make our way through thickets of bracken—a heavy fern—as tall as we are; we exclaim over violets and white lilies that dare to fight for space in this luxuriant undergrowth but avoid touching the creepers that festoon the tall forest trees. We put our palms gently on the emerald green moss and know not to go near the toadstools or mushrooms.

We hike five, ten, and even fifteen miles out, going through dense sholas and steep escarpments and finally stop by one of the many streams that flow clear enough to drink. While cooling our feet in the icy water, we eat our peanut butter sandwiches and watch frogs lay their long streams of eggs in stagnant pools. The boys toss pebbles that have been smoothed by years of flowing water. We identify lantana, maidenhair fern, varieties of mosses, eucalyptus trees, and name the birds that call back and forth to announce our coming; we are proud of our knowledge. Sometimes we even stop for a swim. But we must always return.

Best of all are the camping trips that truly boost our spirits—four giddy days in the marvelous woods. We look forward to these campouts much as American students herald Homecoming Night or the Senior Prom. Our anticipation begins months before the trip, reaching such a crescendo the week before the campouts that teachers no longer try to squeeze any bit of knowledge into our heads. The teachers serve as chaperones on these campouts, so their excitement is most likely of a different sort than ours.

"We have to choose, take a vote or something," the class president says several months before the spring camping trip in our freshman year. "Papa Phelps is waiting for our decision. Where do we want to go?"

"Pumbari," as planned in advance, the girls cry out in unison.

"No, Berigam," insist the boys. "We can swim there."

"Wiffy?" a meek voice comes from the back of the room.

Considerations are the distance to the site, the condition of the tiny government-owned hut in which we will sleep, and the activities offered by the surrounding area—swimming holes rank high.

As we girls are beginning to mature, our criteria for choosing a camp site differ from that of the boys. What we carefully do not reveal is our vision of trysts with one boy or another. The especially dense woods surrounding the hut at Pumbari are perfect for this purpose.

"It's only fifteen miles out," says Joan, who was elected to be our spokesman as she is popular with all of us. "That's an easy hike. We can get there right after lunch; that leaves us the rest of the day for whatever we want."

"Plenty of bracken there. Remember?" chimes in Nell. We always cut armloads of bracken to act as buffer between our bedrolls and the hard floor.

"It's got a front porch," adds Margie. The front porch will allow us occasional freedom from the watchful eyes of our chaperone, who can't be inside and outside at the same time. The boys, although un-suspecting of our motives, are not swayed.

"Leech Shola; it's right down the road, remember?" I play the trump card.

That does it! The boys turn gleeful and quickly set the rules for a contest over whose body will have the most leeches sucking his blood after a tramp through the swamp. The betting begins, most go-ing in favor of Eddie. No bets on Tommy, who has been nervous about everything since the day we put the snake in his desk just to see him jump, scream, and dash for the door. Trysts in the woods are obvi-ously far from the boys' minds.

"I'm taking two pairs of jeans this time," I say later to my room-mates. The campout is still two weeks away, but our bedrolls are already laid out on the floor, ready for stuffing. Whatever we can cram into the bedroll and still roll it up, goes. That and a backpack are all we are allowed.

"If I take a hairbrush, we can share it," Eleanor thinks economically.

"Should I take my best shirts or my worst?" asks Helen. Of course, what will impress the boys is the answer, but will the boys even notice?

The list of essentials is whittled down. Backpack, canteen, tooth brush and paste, socks, a pillow, clothing, and an extra pair of shoes. My Last Doll Peggy must stay behind. How will I sleep? A month ago, hurried letters home begged for funds to purchase any missing items.

"I don't have an extra pair of shoes. Mom wrote that she was sending some; they haven't arrived," complains Muriel. Too late for shoes; these must come from America or be purchased in Madras where the likelihood of finding non-blister-producing shoes is minuscule.

One week before D-Day—Departure Day—we whisper far into the night, wondering about this or that, always fearful of disasters, like whether or not a particular boy will fail to fall in love with us. But the catastrophe that comes is one we have never dreamed of and befalls us this spring, one that is far worse than the end of the world that our fathers promise sinners. And it strikes at our dormitory alone.

"My throat hurts," wails one girl.

Mine too," moans another.

"Oh, no! What about the camping trip?" I cry. "They won't let us go if we're sick." Within hours my fever rises. Soon, instead of talking, I can emit only croaking sounds. This cannot be! I have endured Mr. Musil's horrid Latin class, thinking of the camping trip to come instead of wasting time translating long passages about Rome and the Apian Way. Betty has successfully tutored me through geometry by holding before me the campout as the proverbial carrot. In fact, all the evils of school have been suffered through by virtue of this camping trip. Not go on this trip? I would rather die; my life is over.

In no time, sneezing and fevers abound. "Don't cough on me," the well ones yell, hoping to avoid this epidemic. But it spreads, and now time is perilously running out. We frantically down guava and mango juice, rub our throats with *ichthiol*—black goo made from dead fish and much touted by the nurse—and have our throats painted with iodine. We gargle, spit, and crawl into bed, dispirited.

"If I can just talk normally, maybe I can fake the rest of it," I confess to Joanne. But try as I might, my voice at best is a raspy whisper, at worst nonexistent.

"I'd trade with you if I could. I really would." Joanne can crawl in bed with me when I am frightened by a storm, but she can't rescue me from this calamity.

Two days before the trip, my roommates and I band together. We wipe our noses, suppress the coughs, and make a formal visit to Eagle Eye housemother.

"We are all well enough to go camping," Joanne states this as a fact, just as we have rehearsed it. She is one of the few who has escaped this plague.

"I don't know," Eagle Eye housemother frowns.

"We are just fine. Anyway, that outdoor air is healthy, good for us, the best medicine," another well one speaks her prearranged lines.

"I don't want to be responsible for any one of you catching pneumonia. Imagine what your parents would say," she says. I suppose that admitting to our parents that she has killed us—at least in this fashion—is on her mind. "I know what; I'll just ask Dr. Rosenthal to stop by to make the final decision." We groan and slink away.

Dr. Rosenthal is a small woman, but she is tough, abrupt, and unshakeable. This hurdle would be difficult if one were well, and I am not well. Readying for the doctor's visit, all of us would-be-campers take positions around the living area and try our best to look bright-eyed and healthy. Dr. Rosenthal looks sternly from one of us to another. No reassuring smile, no "I'm on your side here."

"Say ah-h-h," she demands and peers into the first girl's throat, then prods her neck glands. I panic. What am I going to do? I tested my voice before she arrived, and all that came out was a croak. The doctor continues, and I am truly hard pressed.

She is getting closer, now checking Helen, who is sitting on my right. Helen has no voice at all and responds to the doctor's questions in a scratchy, "I'm fine." A dead giveaway if there ever was one.

Then here she is, looking at me, demanding, "Open your mouth wide." My back is to the walls, my fate is about to be sealed. This is a life or death situation and requires all the ingenuity I have ever applied to a difficult situation. I quietly obey, opening my mouth. She gropes for the glands that I have carefully hidden in a high-necked sweater. I simply remain silent. She listens to my chest. I smile politely, saying not a word. She asks if I feel all right, and I nod, still smiling ever so nicely, so sweetly. I hate her. She looks at me long and hard, but I simply continue to beam at her. She sighs and moves on to Joanne, who is seated on my left.

After an eternity, she finishes the rounds. She stands by the door and points to Helen, Margie, and Muriel. "You, you, and you cannot go camping; you are sick!" she booms heartlessly. "The rest of you may go."

I am a Rest of You! I made it! I fooled her, I did! I am like a prisoner whose death sentence has just been commuted.

I watch, wanting this doctor gone, as far away as possible, before I sneeze or cough or make any sound at all. But Eagle Eye housemother fawns over the doctor, thanking her again and again for coming, even offering her tea and cookies. The doctor declines and says she must go. As she walks out the front door, she turns to Eagle Eye and says pointedly, "Gwen was the smart one. She didn't say a word. She kept her mouth shut."

CHAPTER 24

Sin and Redemption

"OUCH," I CRY. The pinprick hurts, but the required amount of blood oozes from my finger. "Your turn." I hand the weapon to my friend Margaret, who seizes it and stabs herself.

"Quickly," she says, "before it dries; before anyone sees us." We press our bloody fingers beside our signatures on the piece of crumpled paper that is carefully laid out on the mossy forest floor.

Together we chant, "I solemnly swear to one deed a day." Our wicked smiles should scare the devil himself.

Huddled in the woods, this oath marks our commitment—not to life-long loyalty to each other or some sort of Godliness—but to sin; one act of depravity to be exercised each and every day for as long as we both shall live, so help me God. Amen.

This bloodshed is necessary. The principal has just denied my request to join the school choir, and revenge is the only recourse. Mom and Dad always take immense joy in my sisters' piano performances and Paul's scholarly achievements, but my report card doesn't look good, and piano practice takes second place to other pursuits.

Mr. Musil was right when he announced to the class the first day, "Gwen, you are the black sheep of your family. You will never make better than a B in Latin."

His frequent shouts of, "Dunderheads!" include me and others who are slow in our translations, conjugations, and word memorization. Outside of class we chant with great enthusiasm, "Latin is a dead language, as dead as dead can be. It killed the ancient Romans, and now it's killing me."

My plan had been to alter my image by singing in the choir. Everyone would see me up there behind the pulpit on Sunday mornings, angelically disguised in a white dress. I could write home about it, make my parents proud just once, and maybe they would even say to others, "Our daughter Gwen, you know, is in the choir at school."

Instead, that pompous principal leaned across his desk, glowered at me, shook his finger, and said tersely, "What business do you have trying to sing in the choir? As it stands, I may have to write a letter to your parents about you. You should be more like your sisters. They make all As. These two Bs are a disgrace to your family!" I shuddered. Being bitten by a cobra or eaten by tigers is better than a letter to my father.

"Let's get even," Margaret had offered the solution.

Determined to seek revenge, I had agreed, "They think I'm so bad; let's show them bad. Break one rule a day, okay?"

We quickly bury the blood-smeared paper underneath our favorite tree in the woods on the hillside below our dormitory. That night we whisper under the covers until the wee hours of the morning, plotting like Ali Baba's thieves. A flashlight illuminates the page on which we laboriously outline the worst possible crimes we can conjure.

No time to waste; we begin the next day. Wreaking havoc permeates our lives, becomes our passion. We are consumed with either committing a wicked deed or designing the next. We skip third period piano practice on a regular basis to devote more time to our mission.

First, we climb the compound wall and visit the bazaar. Although we have no money to spend, freedom is its own opiate. We slip down to the lake on a Sunday afternoon and boldly row a stolen boat in front of the principal's house in the middle of the day. Thrilled with our success, we hide a boat in the afternoon for a dangerous midnight ride. While others are asleep, we steal through the woods, find the craft, and then glide across the beautiful lake in the moonlight. All the while, our ears are keenly tuned for a "Halt!" or "Who goes there?" Yet, only the frogs admonish us.

Time to escalate. A more difficult challenge is to put laxatives in the water jugs in the dining room. This feat involves telling a lie to the nurse to obtain the necessary chemicals and then, when the room is empty, depositing them in the jugs. We laugh uproariously when others push and shove to be first in line at the bathrooms. The servant who empties the toilet buckets goes about her task, muttering in Tamil, a language we don't speak but have no trouble understanding this time.

After lights out, we steal bread from the storeroom attached to the kitchen and generously share it with our roommates. When the cook is blamed for the loss, we feel only slight pangs of guilt. We climb the roof above the cistern and enjoy a cool Saturday afternoon perched on the ledge inside, but nobody notices, although Eagle Eye housefather later mutters about the broken roof tiles. A frog placed in BetterThanThou Sally's bed results in a squish and a cry of horror from us when she inadvertently sits on it. Not a part of the plan. She demonstrates her Christian spirit by piously sleeping with the dead frog until sheet-changing day on Thursday.

"Let's smoke," Margaret challenges me one day.

"We don't have any money," I object, thinking this is a deed beyond forgiveness.

"I saw some in a fancy box in the parlor at the doctor's house. Had to go there once after the dishpan (dispensary) was closed," she explains.

So on Sunday when the dishpan is closed for services, I feign illness and distract the doctor by crying and whining loudly while she administers a generous dose of castor oil. Meanwhile, Margaret surreptitiously stuffs her pockets with the precious loot. We rush back to the woods to sin.

"I'm too young to die," I am afraid to inhale and gostraighttoHell at such an early age.

"Here," Margaret says as she takes a long drag, puts her face to mine, and transfers the smoke into my mouth. I'm convinced this does not truly qualify as smoking, a belief confirmed by the fact that

I don't vaporize instantly and appear at the Pearly Gates to face God on the spot.

Hell fire and brimstone do not rain down on our heads for our wickedness as promised so sternly and so frequently by our parents and the ministers in the pulpits. Ironically, love finally puts an end to our sinfulness. While we are so preoccupied with wreaking havoc, our bodies are quietly doing what young girls' bodies do. We get bumps, curves, and pimples—well, my friends do. All God has given me are fairly good legs and pimples. I'm blind-sided, though, with an extra large ration of falling-in-love, madly in love, never-to-be-forgotten love, the kind we are warned about in church.

I flirt, dream, and lose all caution as I float above the everyday inanities that absorb those not fortunate enough to share the mind-bending experience of unbridled passion. On Sunday I sing "Love divine, all loves excelling, joy of Heaven to earth come down" with such gusto that Joanne elbows me. I don't blush; I am now beyond the restraints of embarrassment, fear, or guilt. Two passions rule my life—desire for My True Love and the wickedness to which I have sworn in blood. In class, I surreptitiously send notes swearing my devotion to My True Love and lists of further schemes to Margaret. After tea, I escape the compound to walk in the woods with My Love and then rush back to plan further sinfulness with my blooded friend.

With all these comings and goings and keeping up with sinning, I am fast approaching overload. The solution? A marriage between the two passions; combine them. It is with this thought that the end begins.

Margaret and I plan the most daring deed ever performed at this boarding school. We will smuggle My True Love into our bedroom at night. T'will break all school records for sin and wickedness. My Love agrees, and the date is set. At the appointed hour, he dutifully knocks at our bedroom window and climbs into our room. We look at him; he looks at us. But our three roommates glare. They want to get into their pajamas, put curlers in their hair, and go to bed. Margaret and I sigh and send him away. But two nights later, a knock at the window and here he is again. I am the only one delighted this time.

Doomed, these trysts die a sudden death that very night. Just as My True Love is retreating, Eagle Eye housefather nabs him. Gossip has it that a letter has been sent to his parents. Margaret and I, meanwhile, are in a tizzy.

"What are they going to do to us?" we ask each other frantically as we wait to hear our fate. But not a word from House Father. For the remaining weeks before winter break, we become saints. We go to bed early, practice the piano, study our lessons—even Latin. Yet, nary a word from Eagle Eye or the principal. No letter from our parents warning of punishments to follow. The tension mounts until, with great relief, we board the train for the three-day trip home for Christmas holidays. We'll be safe there, we are almost certain.

On the hot Indian plains, my sisters, brother, and I sleep until noon or until the crows sit in our windows, cawing for us to rise. Bored, we watch the Indian high school students file through the jackaranda, banana, and guava trees, past the flower garden circled with coconut palms, and across the compound, on their way to school. We sneak over to the students' boarding house in the evenings to eat and practice our Telegu, preferring the students' tasty curry to the American recipes Mother insists on preparing. Late at night Mom feels guilty for all our homesick nights at boarding school, so she wakes us up to sip the hot cocoa she has prepared as a peace offering.

Thus, I am lulled into complaisance by the heat, the dull routine, and Mother's love. All is well. My sins, still unknown to Mom and Dad, are almost forgotten. That is until the awful day when my sisters and I are awakened by loud yelps emanating from the front yard. We rush out to see Father's belt raised over Rajarutnam, an orphaned high school student.

"No, no, please, no, Sahib. I don't want to," Rajarutnam screams, so Father raises his belt and strikes.

Rajarutnum capitulates. "Okay. I'll marry her," but when the pain subsides, he recants. Two or three more strokes of the belt, and

Rajarutnam is resigned to the inevitable. By sneaking over the wall of the girls' dormitory at night to visit orphaned Sugnanama, his True Love, Rajarutnam has committed a sin of such magnitude that Father demands a marriage, immediately; next Sunday at the latest.

My legs turn wobbly with terror. If Dad hears about my secret rendezvous, not over the wall but through the bedroom window, will I be whipped like Rajarutnam, sent back to America by myself, disowned? Or, like Rajarutnum, will I be forced to marry My True Love? My stomach churns, and I feel immense pangs of regret for my wicked ways. I rush to the bathroom, kneel on the cold cement floor, and beg God for deliverance.

Mother makes the wedding preparations for these two orphans who have served our family faithfully as servants for many years, working off their school tuition. A red *sari* for Sugnanama, a white *dhoti* for Rajarutnam, *dundas* of marigolds to adorn their necks, and the ground under the banyon tree in the front yard swept clean. All is ready. I force myself down the steps to observe the ceremony, kiss Sugnanama appropriately, and retreat to the bathroom for more supplication.

My fate becomes clear a few days later when a letter from Mr. and Mrs. Eagle Eye houseparents announces an intended four-day visit to our house. More like four years to me. What am I to do? Will Mr. Eagle Eye expose my secret? Report my misdeeds to my parents? Vacation turns to misery. I spend even more time in the bathroom, pleading God for mercy, but hope is elusive. Romeo and Juliet had it good, I think.

Mom and Dad greet the Eagle Eyes with delight, entertain them, serve them the best curries. While they enjoy long drawn-out afternoon teas, I crouch at the top of the stairs above the dining room to eavesdrop but hear not a word about my sins. No, "Gwen, I have to talk to you," from Dad. Mom does not weep.

I pray, "God, forgive me for my evil doings; I'll study next year, even practice piano if I must. I'll never think about boys or such things again; I promise. Just keep Eagle Eye from telling Dad. Please, God." Should I sign in blood?

The last day of the visit, the last noon meal, and I'm almost home free. Is God answering my prayers? No, such luck. Mr. Eagle Eye housefather and God are not through with me yet.

"Gwen," Eagle Eye clears his throat, "Should I tell your parents about what you've done this past year?"

I freeze. My life hangs in the balance. Can I save myself? I glance at the wedding *dundas* of marigolds that still hang on the wall, then look Heavenward. And sure enough, God comes through, ever present in my time of trouble, just as the preachers promise. I take a deep breath, sit up straight and tall, and give Eagle Eye housefather a piercing look.

More clearly and boldly than I have ever spoken in my life, I make my declaration, "No, you don't need to tell my parents anything. I have asked God to forgive me, and He has!"

Eagle Eye's jaw drops. He has been trumped by God, and he knows it to be so. And that is that. I take a deep breath. It is over. Later that night, lying in bed with my mosquito net tucked safely around me, I reflect on the events of the day and conclude that being the child of a Mennonite missionary sometimes does have its advantages.

CHAPTER 25

Queen for a Day

THE HOLIDAYS PASS too quickly after the Eagle Eyes leave. Goodbyes said once again, and my sisters and I return to the hills, right back to school.

"Rain!" I grin broadly to Margie, my tablemate in Latin class. The clatter on the tin roof is a guillotine beheading instruction. Mr. Musil will have to withhold his attacks on my ignorance until the deluge abates, and that may be a very long time. The din is as thunderous as a freight train roaring down the tracks at eighty miles an hour. No matter how loudly the teachers scream, we can't hear them. Even when we can, we cup our ears and shake our heads, so the teachers frantically wave their arms about, attempting a sort of sign language. They finally resort to writing instructions on the blackboard. With paper being costly and our being poor, written assignments are highly limited, so we are momentarily free. My friends and I think this state of affairs is simply grand.

Saint Betty, my older sister, is actually given the privilege of studying in her dormitory room when it rains. "We don't want you to waste your time just sitting in the classroom," the teachers say sweetly to such an intelligent, trustworthy student. These same teachers don't want either me or my cohorts out of their sight for any reason whatsoever; no use asking.

The yearly monsoon rains are God-sent, rescuing hardworking students like me from the torments of our teachers. We slackers welcome each monsoon season with praise and thanksgiving. No matter that we are pervasively damp from dashing under narrowly covered walkways that stretch from dormitories to the cafeteria, to classrooms, to the gymnasium, or to piano practice rooms at the back of the gym. No matter that we must trot the greater distances to Miss Ruth's bungalow across the compound for piano lessons or, if ill, to the dishpan (dispensary) down the hill. No covered walkways there, so covering our heads with a sweater must do. No, the rain pounding on the tin roofs of the classrooms is a true blessing, every single year.

Down in the hot, dry plains of India, the monsoon rains are also heralded with joy. The dry wells fill; the thirsty fields are satiated; and the wide, earthen tanks dug deep to store water for surrounding villagers accumulate sufficient water for the dry season to come. All a promise of life instead of starvation for the coming year. Monsoon rains are truly glorious all the way around. Yet, the occasional great storms that rage and howl and bring too much moisture in too little time are not welcome. At the end of this school year, my sisters and I learn how unwelcome the storms can be.

Long before the final school bell rings, all of us students are packed and feverish to be gone. The long Christmas holiday is our one and only visit home each year, the trip we have counted down the days for. In light of what is to befall us, we are fortunate that Mother has sent Dad to pick up Betty, Joanne, Margaret, and me and deliver us safely home this year. Paul has already graduated from this school and sailed for America, bound for college where he will begin his preparation to return to India as a missionary himself.

This trip begins as usual. Along with all the other students, our family takes the rickety bus down the mountain to Madurai.

"Goodbye," my friends and I cry at this parting point.

"Write to me; I'll miss you," we urge each other.

"I'll write," we vow again and again. "Do you have my address? Are you sure?" and we double check.

We hug again, shamelessly shed tears, say our umpteenth goodbye, and scatter in various directions on trains that belch soot all over us as they chug into the station and then disappear.

Our family takes the overnight train to Madras where we expect to wait for most of a day for a train to Hyderabad City. Then the final lap to Mahbubnager will bring us home—three days from start to finish is the routine.

But God has other plans for us. In Madras, hawkers shove newspapers in our faces, shouting and pointing to headlines that broadcast news of a tremendous cyclone that has hit the region we are about to traverse.

Dad rushes anxiously to the ticket counter. "Will our train make it through? Should we wait? Take another train, another route?" He is desperate for assurance that we will safely pass through the storm ravaged plains ahead and get home to Mother—and his work, of course.

"Yes, yes. Very, very good, very safe. No problem, no problem. All trains going," is the ticket master's response. Tradition demands that he politely provide a listener with what he wants to hear rather than upsetting him with an unwelcomed truth.

Thus, we soon find ourselves settled comfortably but uneasily in a second class compartment, and the train chugs out of the Madras station. The clickety-clackety-click of the wheels on the tracks lets us know that we are picking up speed. We relax; maybe all will be well after all.

"Check for bedbugs," commands Betty, quickly taking charge, leaving Dad to take care of the worrying.

"I want an upper berth," Joanne insists, and Betty unwillingly claims the other.

No bugs found and sleeping arrangements settled, my sisters and I are free to hang our heads out of the windows, never mind the soot flying back from the engine that quickly infests our hair like lice. We are giddy with delight over our freedom, and like fickle lovers, we quickly forget the sorrow of parting from our friends.

We chug along for only a few hours before the train slows. "Look, look," I say needlessly. We are surrounded by devastation—flooded rice fields and trees with roots pointed skyward.

By mid-afternoon the train slows to a crawl; the waters now lap up against the tracks.

"Can we open the door?" Joanne asks eagerly.

"Okay," Dad says, "But be careful." So Joanne, Betty, and I squeeze into the open doorway and sit with our bare feet dangling over the edge, toes dangerously close to the water.

"Watch for snakes," Dad warns. We quickly draw our feet up and rest our elbows on our knees. We are horrified, yet mesmerized, by the sight of melting mud huts floating by with entire families clinging to the soggy, thatched roofs. The men's eyes speak quiet resignation; mothers clutch their terror stricken children. Water covers the land as far as we can see and all is silent except for the ever-slowing, chug-chug of the engine.

"Here, we'd better eat before it gets too dark," Dad hands out the curry puffs we purchased at the last minute in Madras. The food is barely past our lips, though, when the train's wheels squeal, the engine belches a last gasp, and we come to a complete halt.

"Dad," I cry, "What's happening? I'm scared." Margaret huddles quietly against me. But Dad doesn't answer, so we just wait expectantly for some sort of forward motion, straining for a reassuring hiss from the engine.

Instead, the engineer bangs on our compartment door. Between his Tamil mixed with some broken English, Dad's Telegu, and much waving of arms, we understand that the bridge up ahead has washed away. The engineer indicates that we must get out and walk. He assures us that we can safely traverse what remains of the bridge and eventually reach a small town about a mile down the track. Dad conveys his concern about leaving our luggage behind, so the engineer rounds up a few coolies. Dad supervises the hoisting of our trunks onto the collies' shoulders, and we carefully begin our trek.

Some fearful passengers choose to remain on the train rather than risk life and limb. They hang out the windows and doors, shouting back and forth in various languages with each other and the engineer. Others move cautiously toward the bridge, one hand on the train to steady themselves while hollering advice to those ahead and behind. Every man has the perfect solution to our predicament, but nobody listens, so the volume and urgency increases to an almost unbearable din. The women carry hastily bundled belongings on their heads and keep up an endless stream of orders to their wide-eyed, frightened children who cling to their mother's *saris*. The women loudly accuse their husbands of deviously planning this disaster and screech at one another to move more quickly.

Reaching the bridge, we find that only one rail remains, and it is fastened precariously to a few boards. We creep forward in the darkness, depending on the moon and a small lantern that the engineer waves about to light the way.

"Don't look down," Dad shouts as we tiptoe across. I look down. Only blackness looms below, but the rushing water needs no illumination to remind us of the danger. Following right behind us, each coolie tips and sways, one arm waving wildly for balance, the other clutching the baggage entrusted to him. Upon reaching the opposite shore, passengers and coolies bunch together in relief, but urged forward by the engineer, all trudge forward, watching carefully for snakes or other vermin seeking high ground and a bite out of our skin. I keep my eye on Dad, his tall figure my only reassurance this dark night.

"I'm glad that Mom sent Dad for us," I say to Joanne.

"What would we have done by ourselves?" she whispers.

Overhearing, Dad says, "God works in mysterious ways." I have to agree this time.

The mile promised by the engineer is more like two, but we finally reach the train station, where we are met by the ticket master. Noting the color of our skin, he indicates that some missionaries live on the far edge of town. We quickly store our heavy trunks in his office and wake a slumbering driver huddled in the dirt beside his *jutka*. He whips his skinny, weary horse into action and hustles us off to the mission compound. No matter that these missionaries are Lutheran, given our circumstances, we don't care if they are Catholic or Hindu. Even at this dreadfully late hour, these kind folks lovingly take us in, feed us, and make up beds for the night. This certainly should earn them a seat in Heaven, I think.

The next morning Dad sends a telegram to Mom telling her we are safe, not to worry; we'll get home as soon as possible. Without radio, newspaper, or telephone, her means of gleaning bits of news about the storm is limited to what the servants bring in from town, much garbled and embellished upon. Our telegram likely sends her mind racing with all sorts of speculations that will escalate, twist, and turn by the hour. We, on the other hand, wait for hours until a train comes from the north to carry us the rest of the way to Hyderabad City. After another wait, another night, and another train, we make the final leg to Mahbubnager and home.

Dark has settled by the time a *jutka* picks us up from the station. Joanne and I are too tired to fight or even complain, so weary that the clip clop of the horse's hooves almost puts us to sleep before we reach the mission compound. Mother rushes out to hug us and then cries, then hugs us again, and then cries again. She holds her lantern up high to inspect every inch of us. Our bodies and hair are black with soot from hanging out train windows, but she takes no notice.

"I was so worried," she sobs, "I've waited and waited, heard so many stories. I didn't know…didn't know if you were alive. Oh, my. Oh, I'm so happy." Waiting all alone for days, she has heard sporadic and unverifiable reports of death and destruction wrought by the storm and had plenty of time to believe her worst nightmares have come true. She had convinced herself that we had all perished, despite Dad's telegram to the contrary.

She quickly rouses the servants and directs them to bring us some supper. Meanwhile, my sisters and I, now fully awake, eagerly help Dad recount the tale of our perilous journey, feeling free to exaggerate here and there.

Mother interrupts occasionally, "Oh, I'm so happy. You're all safe, safely home!" and she hugs us again. She is so pleased to see us that I begin to puff up with pride at just being alive!

When all that needs to be said is, she notices the soot. "My, how dirty you are! Your hair! You have to have a bath, every one of you; you can't get into bed like this."

My sisters and I pick up lanterns and make our way upstairs to where the bathroom counter is lined with a half dozen *kujas* of water that the servants have filled at the well and carried up the outside steps. Behind the counter the floor slants toward a drain where we stand and pour umpteen dippers of water over ourselves, lathering our hair about three times before the water runs clean. I reach for a towel but stop in astonishment. I can only stare for a moment because there on the rack are large, fluffy towels, the savedonlyforcompany towels—pink, blue, white, and yellow. I am struck speechless by the obvious depth of Mother's concern for us, her children. These save-donlyforcompany towels tell me ever so clearly—even more than all her tears, hugs, and kisses—how much she has worried about us and how much she really, really, truly, deeply loves us. I reach for the pink towel and soak up not only water drops but Mother's love as well. This, I think, must be what it is like to be a queen.

My sisters and I sleep until noon the next day, so tired we are not even wakened by the crows perched on the verandah railing, caw-ing for the world to join them. Hungry again but groggy with sleep, I make my way to the bathroom and look expectantly for the fit-for-a-queen towels, wanting to wrap myself once more in their loving embrace and luxuriate in the memory of Mother's love.

I stop short, fully awake now. The towels are gone, replaced with the old, worn thin, everyday towels. My heart sinks. I know the com-pany towels have already been washed and packed away in a trunk downstairs beside the smooth, white, folded sheets that smell like America, ready for the real guests when they come. I also know that things are already back to normal, and Mother's uncontrolled and lavish demonstrations of love are probably packed away as well. I stare at the old towels. The love just hasn't lasted long enough for me.

In no time flat, like the worn towels, our familiar being-at-home routine sets in. Yet occasionally when I lie in bed at night with the mosquito net tucked in around me, I watch the flickering light of the lantern and unwrap, like a present, the wonderful memory of being a queen for one whole day.

Drawing Water from the Well

CHAPTER 26
The Black Umbrella

AT FIRST WE think that our worst problem will be coats. But in the end, it isn't. Evidently God has called our family to return to America, even if our seven years aren't up yet. To be president of a Mennonite College is where God wants Dad to be now. God can't seem to get it straight. Are we to be here or over there?

After the wild ride home courtesy of the cyclone and after some boring weeks on the mission compound, my sisters and I are ready to go back to school. School is where we have all sorts of wonderful friends, a mixture of Methodists, Presbyterians, Lutherans, and a variety of others, even some whose parents are not missionaries but work for a government agency or for large companies based in this part of the globe. But what my friends' parents do doesn't matter to me one bit. I am also madly interested in some of the boys. It would be easier to take a starving baby's bottle from her mouth than rip me from my friends.

As usual, God pays me no mind. So here it is January, and instead of packing our trunks to go back to school, we are suddenly bound for a Mennonite settlement in Kansas. No warning—answer The Call, just go, right now, forget about finishing the school year, doesn't matter.

"This will be a learning experience. You can catch up on Latin and Algebra later," Dad rationalizes. He has planned a month's detour through Europe.

"But we have no coats," my sisters and I complain to Mom. "How are we to travel through Europe in the dead of winter without coats?"

Even if we had coats, we certainly don't have those "shortie" coats that we hear is all the rage in the States. Having never seen one, we concoct the notion that shortie coats mean cut mid-thigh, below the pockets, and certainly should not meet our ankles. We are desperate for coats, and they must be fashionable.

No need to worry—God and the Mennonite church in Minnesota come through once again. A missionary barrel has arrived just in the nick of time. In the large, black metal drum with *J.N.C. Hiebert, Mahbubnager, South India* painted on the side, we find red, long-handled underwear. We quickly donate the ugly thing to the coolie who daily draws our water from the well. He shows up the next day decked out in that red underwear and nothing else. He struts about, then proudly pulls up the water bucket, splashing his new garb in the process; now he looks all spotted. The missionary barrel holds used dresses, blouses, underwear, and to our delight, coats of many colors! Why would anyone send coats to southern India where a dip to seventy degrees sends natives scurrying to construct large bonfires for warmth?

Dad smiles and says, "You see, don't you, that God works in mysterious ways?" We have to agree.

The coats, though, are long and certainly not in style. No problem. We get out the scissors and deftly shorten the coats to what we assume is a stylish length although they are still fitted at the waist. The pockets now reside near the hem.

"Mine's done," boasts Betty, so Joanne and I work feverishly to catch up.

"Mom, what are you going to wear?" I ask.

"This one," she holds up a full-length, blue coat. "It's just the way I want it, long and warm." She doesn't have time for this cutting-off-coats foolishness.

"But Mom, we'll be so embarrassed," I wail. But neither she nor Margaret nor baby Lois care one bit about fashion.

It all happens in a hurry. Most of our belongings are doled out to other missionaries who are happy for our cast-off dishes, bedding, and furniture. Our cook, though, is the most highly prized of what we claim ownership to, so Mom sends him to our cousins, the Wiebes. The few items we will take are packed into a couple of worn suitcases. I hold My Last Doll Peggy tightly to my chest and cling to a worn suitcase about the size of Dad's briefcase.

"Mom, this has all my doll's clothes in it. Can't I take it? I'll carry it myself," I plead.

"No. Dad says just these few bags; that's all," and Peggy's vast, lovingly hand-sewn wardrobe is left in a corner.

"For the rats," I mutter bitterly.

With our white-washed mission bungalow as a backdrop, we hastily pose for parting pictures under the low-hanging banyan trees out front. Pictures with our cook, the household staff, church pastors, the Indian high school students, then the elementary students, those who live on the compound and those who don't, and on it goes, everyone eager to be in a picture and be remembered for eternity. Pictures that we will peer at years later and be unable to put names to the faces. Our necks are garlanded with *dundas,* necklaces fashioned from hundreds of marigolds gathered from the fields at dawn. Even the car is decked with strings of flowers. Tears follow picture taking, but finally we must leave.

Hanging halfway out the windows, we wave our last goodbyes, thinking we are off. But Dad stops to rush back for one last check of the house. Sure enough, we left something behind. My doll's clothes? No such luck. Grinning broadly, he bounds back down the steps, one hand firmly grasping the *topee* that shades his head from the hot sun, the other carrying a large, black umbrella that he thrusts into the back seat.

"Can't leave this!" he says triumphantly. We push the umbrella out of sight under the seat, completely unaware of the significance of this fleeting event.

As we board our ship in Bombay, I drag the umbrella behind me as we make our way up the gangplank and shove it under the bunk from which I will moan and vomit for most of the next two weeks. The umbrella? Forgotten until Dad retrieves it when we dock in London.

We shiver and shake as we go from one sight to another, our shortie coats keeping us warm only to our thighs. Our cotton dresses provide little warmth in the space between the coat's hem and the top of our socks. Our sturdy, brown, tie shoes, though, keep our toes from frostbite.

"Look how unfashionable these women are," Betty points to the British women who rush about in the cold wind, pinching together the fronts of their coats, coats that reach down to their ankles. We scoff.

"You'd think they'd know more about fashion, being so close to France!" I chime in, completely puzzled by what we see. "Oh well, at least we have shortie coats. We are in style."

Dad has the trip well planned. "We'll go sightseeing during the day and sleep on trains at night—saves money." And wherever we go, the umbrella goes too.

Now, this is not a dainty, napkin-size American umbrella printed with daisies and trimmed in ruffles. Rather, it is designed to keep one dry in Indian monsoons when the sky lets loose with torrential rains that last for weeks. The umbrella is taller than I am and large enough around for at least three of us to eat lunch under. It certainly does nothing to stave off this bone-chilling cold.

Dad assigns sole responsibility for the umbrella to Betty, Joanne, and me. For a few days, we tote the gargantuan old fossil through museums and drag it with us when we travel the underground. We can't even eat without it poking our ankles. Our aversion to the umbrella grows by the hour as does our embarrassment at being seen with it. People stare at us, point, and shake their heads—has to be the umbrella. We fight over the hated responsibility until Betty declares that we will simply take turns. Thus we will each endure embarrassment for one day, followed by a two-day reprieve. For those two reprieve days, I trail at least twenty feet behind the family, a teenage girl in a cut-off coat, no gloves, in worn, brown tie-shoes, and a cotton dress, pretending not to be associated in any way with that strange-looking family or the ugly umbrella. I think I have fooled everyone.

But it is too much! Angrily, Betty, Joanne, and I begin to plot. The umbrella has become an albatross from which we must be freed. We surreptitiously hang it near the instruments of torture in the Tower of London, but Dad spies it just as we are about to leave. Seasick all the way across the English Channel, we slip it under our blankets and moan loudly when Dad comes near.

Nevertheless, upon disembarking, Dad counts the bags and shouts, "Where's the umbrella? Get it!"

We hang the ugly thing on a rack amidst the coats in an Amsterdam restaurant, but as we leave, Dad points at us and shouts, "The umbrella!"

One of our infrequent hotel stays is in a hotel in Luzerne, Switzerland. Joanne, Betty, and I search frantically for hiding spots.

"Look," I whisper, "here's a little closet, right here behind the door. It goes to the attic. He'll never see it."

"Great," Joanne is pleased as her turn is next. She grins, "Dad always says that God answers prayers."

"Let's have a funeral for it," I suggest, pleased that we have finally found a final resting place for the umbrella. We stash it and spend the next two days joyfully seeing the sights and tramping up and down snow-covered hillsides—in our fashionable shortie coats, of course. We almost make it. Dad pays the bill, and like sardines in a can, we cram all of ourselves into one taxi.

But just as the driver pulls out, Dad barks, "Where is the umbrella?"

"Your turn," groans Betty. Everyone has to climb back out of the cab so that I, at the bottom of the pile, can get out and climb back up the stairs to disinter the umbrella.

Betty, Joanne, and I are now tightly bonded in our quest, slightly discouraged but not completely daunted. We leave that hideous millstone in the ladies' bathroom on the railroad express in Germany, but when we disembark, Dad counts heads and baggage and yells, "Gwendolyn, where is the umbrella?" I slink back to retrieve it. We hide it under a tomb in a museum, but Dad is right behind us, "Pick up that umbrella!" he hisses. We lay it to rest near the stone where Mary Queen of Scots lost her head. All to no avail. Just when we think we have seen its last, Dad turns and demands that we retrieve our shackle.

One final stop—the Mennonite Central Relief Center in Germany. This stark place is where refugees languish after being smuggled in from Russia in the dark of night, sometimes staying for years in large Quonset huts, waiting for papers that never come. Gaunt, dreary people in tattered clothing silently watch us as we pass. Their homes are army blankets hung for walls. One blanket deep and one blanket wide provides quarters for an entire family. No place to hide a large umbrella here!

"Kneel," Dad commands, "Let's pray for these poor folks." With refugees for an audience, Dad speaks to God in German, asking for deliverance from this place for these sad people. All I want is out of here!

Just as we leave, a young woman chases us down, thrusts a package of mittens, woolen stockings, and knitted caps into Mom's hands and mutters something about feeling sorry for us, that we look like we need help. Joanne, Betty, and I look each other up and down in surprise; for the first time we see ourselves as others might. Old brown tie shoes, worn socks, thin cotton dresses, and cut-off coats—perhaps we aren't as stylish as we thought.

Late in January of 1952, we sail from France on the largest passenger ship of the early 1950s, the *Ile De France,* but even there we find no way to disengage Dad from his obsession with the umbrella. Nor do we have any luck on the train trip from New York to Grandma's house in Minnesota. The black umbrella has toured the world!

Grandma lives upstairs, taking up the entire space above Grandpa's large hardware store, the village's main shopping attraction. All the relatives have gathered to greet us.

"Here," Grandma says, pointing to a hall closet, "Put your coats in here. Then come to the kitchen; I've got *borscht,* you're hungry, yes?" Hunger is an assumption German grandmothers make. And we'd better eat it all.

We stash our shortie coats and the umbrella in the closet and join the grand celebration. Uncle John has supplied gallons of ice cream, others have brought pickles, pies, apples, ham—all those goodies we have longed for and done without. These relatives also bring cast-off clothing, including their old, long coats. To my surprise, these cousins wear long coats themselves. Like the British, they seem unaware of the latest styles. Perhaps Minnesota winters bring you to survival level, I think.

We visit all around for a week or so, say goodbye, and make our way to Kansas. Must not forget The Call.

It isn't until Easter that our notions about shortie coats are set straight. On this Sunday, according to custom and without warning to us, the Kansas girls launch their Spring Wardrobes. Their winter clothes, now in distain, are discarded overnight, like the skins that snakes used to shed over our doorways while we slept. Still garbed in our winter clothing, Betty, Joanne, and I are so embarrassed we could crawl under a pew and rot. The girls don't even try to hide their giggles; the women turn their heads away to hide their pity. We sit alone in shame, aware now that Easter Sunday is the day when winter wardrobes of wool or corduroy or heavy rayon are exchanged for entirely new, summer gowns of cotton, wispy gauze, and even silk. The God of Wardrobes has deserted us.

The other girls sport bright, flowered dresses, white shoes, and new, pastel colored coats—the short ones we have so emulated. These beautiful coats are cut on the bias so that they flair in the back, can be flipped from side to side with a twitch of the shoulders, and end just above these girls' dainty fingertips, not mid-thigh. Without darts, the coats are loose-fitting and have pockets hidden high in the side seams, almost under their armpits.

Well, all right. Our estimations were wrong, but we can do this. Betty, Joanne, and I rush to purchase some lightweight wool and once again get out the scissors. We'll get it right this time.

Several years later, on one of our numerous visits to Grandma's house, we climb the stairs and stop to hang our coats in the hall closet before entering the parlor where Grandma is ensconced in her rocking chair, waiting for us. I grab for a hanger and spy something dark and musty in the far recesses of the closet. Gingerly, I reach in and pull it out. It can't be, but it is. The big, black umbrella, right where it has been all this time since we first arrived from India.

CHAPTER 27

Revelations

WE HAVE PING ponged back and forth between America and India, and now the ball makes its final stop in Kansas. Once again I ask myself the same, tired questions. Why are we here, then there, and back again? Why the many separations? Don't we belong somewhere?

Everything is different here in Kansas, right from the start. This is not at all like the Promised Land of America that we longed for all those years in India. I think that maybe just this one time God made a mistake, a big one, got the wrong number or something when He sent The Call for Dad to come to this community and become the president of their small Mennonite College.

Betty, Joanne, and I object to this place on several counts. First, this place is ugly—no mountains, streams, valleys; just wheat fields so flat we can stand in one place and see the grain elevators of four different towns by just turning around. Now, that's flat! Then there is the fact that the Mission Board's office is here. Consequently, we have frequent encounters with the grim men who have decided where we will go, when we will go there, what we will do when we get there, and how much money we need. If it isn't enough, too bad. Go without, smile and say thanks anyway. God sends The Call; the Mission Board does the rest.

This town is also where our family once left Phyllis and Grace behind to attend college while we went off to save souls. In that dark hour, these two oldest sisters—my extra mothers—stood with arms about each other and sobbed as we waved and waved, even after we lost sight of them. We sat mute with pain, knowing we wouldn't see them again until God and the Mission Board sought fit to bring us back.

Dad's new job here in Kansas pays him more money than we have ever seen. Yet he and Mom argue its distribution. "We need furniture, beds, a sofa, a larger table and more chairs," Mom says, "and the children need clothing." No missionary barrels here for us to raid; besides, we aren't missionaries any more so don't rank as ThoseWhoAreInNeed.

"We have to have a car," Dad insists that the old borrowed vehicle must be returned and soon. "I have to have a new suit for the job. You know my black suit is in bad shape. Can't show up in my old khakis either." She can't argue with that.

I have two skirts and three blouses, compliments of my Minnesota cousins. When I mix and match mine with Joanne's equally sparse wardrobe, I can sport a wide variety of outfits—a rich wardrobe by India boarding school standards. I immediately learn that such an accumulation of clothing is subpar by American standards. Teenage girls here seem to have an endless supply of clothing, a different dress every day for at least two weeks—underwear too, I bet, and no need to share. These girls strut about in fluffy sweaters, crinoline petticoats, skirts with ruffles, peddle-pushers for after school, and jeans for weekends. They chew an endless supply of gum, drink cokes, wear lipstick, and some girls even frequent the beauty shop. These pampered girls have saddle shoes as well as loafers for weekdays, high heels for Sundays.

Betty, Joanne, and I hold hands and cry every day as we walk home from the local high school. Nobody here appreciates that we can read Shakespeare, compute advanced geometry, and have personal experience with the geography of the whole wide world. They don't offer Latin in this Kansas school; just typing for boys and home economics for girls. "To prepare you for life," the principal says proudly as he signs me up.

When Betty asks the teachers about homework, one laughs and says, "We don't do that here." Another advises, "Lighten up. Have a good time."

Good time? No hills to climb, no forests to explore, no taffy pulls or skating parties, no Methodist or Presbyterian friends to share a dormitory room, secrets, or clothing with; not even homework to avoid.

What people mostly do here in Mennonite Kansas is go to church. Sunday mornings, folks get all gussied up and appraise each others' finery. The one-hour sermon follows an hour of Sunday School. Sunday evening? Church again. Wednesday night? Church. Thursday night? A change-up—choir practice. I long for the Sunday night moonlit walks around the lake after vespers, Saturday night movies, and weekend camping trips. Even those dreadful, everynightoftheweek study halls take on a touch of glamour.

In the beginning, our dearth of clothes bothers me the most. But as the song says, "Through many dangers, toils, and snares, I have already come." I've looked Eagle Eye Housefather straight in the eye to save myself from Dad's wrath, climbed tall mountains, and crossed dangerous oceans—I surely can handle this. I stand up straight, and declare that if brains aren't the major game in town, I am up to the new challenge.

During the school year, I find a house-cleaning job—fifty cents every Saturday. With cloth at twenty-five cents a yard, I can sew at least one skirt, blouse, or even a dress every single week. The next summer, with more time on my hands, I advance to working in the local Old Folks' Home, where my paternal grandparents are ending their days. For forty cents an hour, I walk the mile there, set the tables for breakfast, serve the upstairs bedridden folks their trays, clear and wash all the dishes, peel potatoes, wash the vegetables, set the table and serve trays again, wash the lunch dishes, and after the cook leaves, mop the floor. Seven in the morning until one in the afternoon, six days a week.

Sometimes my grandmother says, "Here, let me help you," and hands me dishes, helps set the tables, and even dries some of the mounds of dishes I must clean. Before she goes back upstairs to care for Grandpa, we take a short break and have a little visit.

This Grandma is a tiny, even frail woman, with thinning gray hair pulled back in a bun. Yet she has a calm strength about her. She is so unlike my Minnesota grandmother who weighs three-hundred pounds and enjoys a good old fashioned argument. Too much alike, she and I are forever pulling at opposite ends of whatever Tug-of-War game we have going. In contrast, my Kansas grandmother and I talk quietly and without urgency, slowly forming a tenuous bond between us.

This Old Folks Home work is harder than hiking ten miles for a picnic. When I get home each day, my spent, prone body lies motionless for hours in front of our window air conditioner in the living room. The carrot that keeps me going, though, is the dreams of all the clothes I will be able to make with the money I am saving.

By the end of summer, an insidious change has crept into me without my even knowing. My appreciation for knowledge and intellectual pursuits has withered in proportion to my increasing desire for amassing worldly goods. Turned Scrooge, I frequently count my savings.

"I'll even have money left over for shoes and some of those fluffy sweaters the other girls wear," I confide to Joanne, whose envy knows no bounds. "I'll share, you know that," I add quickly, unlike Scrooge.

Not missing the work, but missing my grandmother, I announce one winter day, "I'm going to go see Grandma. I haven't been there in a while."

"I have just one request," Dad stops me at the door. "Take off that lipstick; it would upset her." I have just recently worn him down enough to gain permission to use the dab of makeup these Mennonites have voted off their much touted Sins List. Still desperate to fit in, I need the red lips.

"Fine," I say and rub my lips vigorously before making the trek across town. I still don't know this grandma very well. These grandparents probably posed for The American Gothic. Austere, unsmiling, ever so severe, they have endured what the church ladies call A Hard Life. As malaria ridden missionaries, they returned to the harsh life of Minnesota farming so that Grandpa could travel from town to town and continue to save souls. Their final stop? This Kansas Old Folks Home.

I find Grandma sitting in her rocking chair, knitting a small afghan. "For old people in wheelchairs, to keep their legs warm," she explains as though she herself isn't old yet. Work, work, work. If there is none available, she will invent something, just to keep busy. She can't stop, not even now.

We exchange pleasantries, and then I say impulsively, "Grandma, tell me about being a missionary."

So she recounts the time in the late 1800s when she and Grandpa made the six-weeks voyage to India and traveled in areas where no white man had ever been seen. She tells about struggling with the language and living in a mud hut until their home was built, about burying a baby, and finally succumbing to malaria.

"We had to come back, we were too sick," she says. "We didn't get finished with God's Work; just got started, really."

"Does that bother you?" I ask, the seed of insight beginning to form way down inside of me as the why questions bubble up once again.

She doesn't answer; I'm not sure she has heard me.

"Yes," she says finally. "It did. But God had other plans."

"Tell me about my dad," I probe, more and more comfortable with her, given the thread of kinship we have woven over the past summer.

"I know," I list the names of her children, my aunts and uncles. This much I do know about her unusual family.

She talks proudly about her children's many accomplishments—Uncle Alvin's gift for mathematics that earned him a position in the "Think Tank" in California, Uncle Sam's fortitude and bravery in the army, Uncle Lando's touching sermons in a large church here in town, and about the aunts who became nurses and teachers.

"Your father was always so intense, pushing himself. We were so proud when he received The Call to go to India." She pauses and then adds, "He was in the middle." She smiles again, "Like you."

"I hate being in the middle," I confess. "I'm never as good as the others. Phyllis, Betty, Paul, Joanne, they get straight As, play the piano, never get in trouble. Paul's even going to be a missionary, did you know?" She does.

"I think Dad is disappointed in me. I know he is." I have never voiced this thought but now know it to be true. "I'd like to please him; I think I do anyway."

Grandma thinks this over for a moment. "Maybe your dad once thought that too, when he was young," a new thought for both of us. Is this a piece that fits my puzzle? One answer?

"Do you suppose that is why he went to India? I know he says that God called him, but do you think . . . ?" This borders on heresy, yet she doesn't chastise me. Instead we sit in silence together, chewing on the thought that Dad, like me, had once wanted to please his parents, that India might have been the answer.

When I get home, Dad asks, "How was the visit?' I look at him, not seeing the dad that I left an hour ago but an ordinary sort of man. I thought he was taller, and I almost say so.

Instead, I say, "Fine. No-o. Better than fine. I like this grandma. I think I'll visit her more."

"Good," he is pleased.

I hesitate and then look him straight in the eye, something rare for me. "Dad, you had to finish what Grandma and Grandpa started, didn't you? In India."

He is startled by the question. He pauses, seeming to twist this notion about. Then slowly, as if he also has found a missing puzzle piece, he says. "Maybe I did. Maybe so." Then, catching himself, he hastily adds, "Of course, God called me."

"I know all that," I say, "but it's more than that. You wanted to go."

"Yes," he admits, "I did. Actually, ever since I was young." He thinks for a moment, going back in time. "Actually, we were supposed to go to Africa, were all prepared for that, but then, at the last minute, the opening in India came up. So that's where the mission board sent us, but India is where I really wanted to be. And where God wanted me to be." He smiles, "It all worked out."

"Well," I say firmly, "I'm not going to go to India like Paul is. Or Africa either. I don't want to be a missionary or anything like that at all." Yet I just can't help myself from adding, "You know, Dad, I might just become a Methodist or something. Some day."

CHAPTER 28

Full Circle

WHILE THIS ACCOUNT of one Mennonite missionary's daughter might seem to end here, the story does not actually come full circle for many years. A long time and many stories later, after the death of my father, my marriage, the births of my lovely children, and after those children are half grown, I summon the courage to fulfill a long-delayed dream. I want to return to the intellectual pursuits that I once valued as a child but that slipped away when I went through the contortions necessary to fit into an American society to which I did not belong. I want to complete my college education.

For a few years after that truly glorious day when a coveted degree is finally bestowed upon me, I find that teaching fifth graders is the most exciting thing since sliced bread. Yet it doesn't take long before I grow bored and am jumping at the bit to be the one at the top, run a school my own way although my only experience in giving orders is to my students and to my own children who, after all, are turning out pretty well, if I do say so myself. So I continue to trek across town to the university until I have what they say I need to become The Boss—a school administrator. Recalling my past, I take a moment to look up to the skies, remember those years in boarding school, and promise God that I will be a loving and kind boss, never tyrannical, never mean.

Degree in hand and the third little pig as my model, I travel to a mid-size Texas town and sit primly in the district superintendent's office, looking pretty nifty in my new pink suit and artificially blonded hair.

I tell the superintendent about myself, my background, and my experiences as a fifth grade teacher. I recount my years as school counselor and my current job as an assistant principal in a nearby district. I answer his questions with my head held high and look him straight in the eye. After facing housefathers, stormy seas, cobras, and scorpions, this is easy. This game I like to play.

"I want to be a principal," I say.

"Why?" he throws back.

"I want to make a difference," I give the standard response.

Then he jumps right in with the hard stuff, goes for the jugular. "What will you do to win over the community?"

So I talk about how I will sing in the Methodist Church choir, and tell him about my plan to show my father's missionary slides of India to any local group that will have me. He looks at me sharply when I mention missionarying and then seems to mentally file that away.

He moves on to the nitty-gritty of it all, daring me to falter, "What will you do if a student brings a gun to school, or a knife, becomes violent? What if a parent threatens you?"

No problem. He doesn't know about wicked housefathers, or doctors who might not let me go camping, or Latin teachers who call me the black sheep of the family, much less having snakes shed their skins over the doorways while I sleep nearby. I rise to the challenge and easily provide all the correct answers.

Finally comes the question I really want to hear, "Would you like to see the school, the one that needs a principal?" We drive through the town to first view the local businesses that provide the district's tax base and hopefully my salary as well. I see a very clean, brick school building with a flag waving merrily out front. For me, I think.

He clears his throat, "Ah-h, that's not the one." We pass some costly homes with green lawns and white folks fastidiously washing expensive cars in their driveways. "Ah-h, this isn't the area," he says. We cross the railroad tracks and with each passing block, more and more potholes decorate the streets and the houses appear more dingy, falling down even. People, mostly shades of black and brown, sit on porches or slouch on doorsteps or broken down sofas, chatting and watching poorly clad children play in the streets. All the activity stops when we pass; they stare at us, the white folks in the shiny black car. The superintendent grows silent. We make a right and then a left and stop in front of a low, yellow-bricked school. Empty beer bottles, plastic trash bags, and cigarette butts camouflage the few scrawny bushes that have survived severe abuse. The front door may have been red at one time, but the paint is faded to a peeling pink.

The superintendent nervously clears his throat. "Well, ah-h, here we are." He sees the squalor and debris, a school that matches its surroundings. But I see a school that could be my very own. Mine to love and cherish to my heart's content, if I play my cards right.

The door creaks as we go inside. In contrast to the outer wrappings, though, the halls are shiny clean and walls newly painted. I am preoccupied, wondering how I can persuade this man that I am the person for this job—a 49-year-old, inexperienced, but very eager woman.

We step into the tiny outer office where the secretary, maybe my secretary—I've never had my own secretary—will sit crowded into a corner between file cabinets, a computer, time cards, typewriter, stacks of folders, and bulging boxes stacked to the ceiling. The superintendent leads the way into an inner office. Will this become my office? He sees a tiny room with a desk and a chair, two file cabinets, some shelves, and room for nothing more. I see blue walls that match my blue sofa; I see the shelves filled with my books and treasured collection of colorful dolls from around the world; and I imagine the room adorned with my pictures of children from the various nations I have visited. The large window that overlooks a courtyard strewn with beer bottles, broken glass, and trash of all sorts is instantly transformed into a window that overlooks a grassy knoll.

I smile and sigh. I am home. I belong here; I know it to the very core of my being.

The superintendent and I return to his spacious, sparkling clean, plush office, a sharp contrast to the scene we just left. He wants to verify my willingness to take on this daunting job.

"There is almost no turnover in faculty at this school," he says. "That needs to change." This means that some teachers need to be fired.

"The principal that left had a farm to tend to on the side," meaning that that principal closed his door and slept most afternoons.

"Test scores are low here and absolutely must improve." This means teachers need help. And so the conversation goes. He almost dares me to walk away, but I am undaunted. I want this school more than anything else in the world.

The superintendent returns to that filed-away thought, "You say that your father was a missionary?" He doesn't say it but means, "I hope you inherited that missionary spirit because you are going to need it."

Then he asks the last question, the one which he could have dispensed with at the outset and saved himself a lot of trouble, "Do you want the job?"

Do I want the job? I do a couple of mental handsprings and somersaults. "Yes," I say firmly, "I want the job." What I really mean is, "I would die for the job, pay me what you want, and I want to start tomorrow, maybe even today."

He walks me to the door. "Well, I'll bring your name before the school board Tuesday night, but I don't think there will be any trouble; they will most likely accept it." This means, "We are desperate; they'll jump at the chance."

I walk down the hall and out the front door. I drive back to the school of my dreams and get out. I look around and then up at the sky. I think that I can see God and my Father holding hands up there, and they are laughing. I can't help but join in. The Calls my Father received so mysteriously and so frequently, The Calls that so often left me confused and angry have come right to my own front door. This most beautiful school in the world is my very own mission field, one that makes my heart beat faster, fills me with dreams and hopes. I have received *My Call*.

What Became of Us

IN THE YEARS since our family's final return from India, my sisters, brother, and I have come to appreciate the past we shared. The unusual life we led as children of missionaries, the rigorous academic education we received at boarding school in those beautiful hills, and our parents' strong religious values resulted in our leading honest, fairly productive lives. Each of us placed a high value on education, and all found avenues to be of service to others. Interestingly, most of us left the Mennonite faith, yet each of us raised our children with good old-fashioned Mennonite values.

For myself, I am now in the ranks of those living in the time God reserves for reflection. I sit contentedly on my porch and—like the slowly rising spring bulbs in my garden—from my unconscious and then to my conscious thinking, comes the startling realization that being Mennonite cannot actually be shed like a snake discards its skin. It seems that I can't lie, would rather die than steal, and am finally comfortable with my life-long partner—guilt. I feel righteous sitting in my church pew, still think that hymns should make one cry when thinking of dead relatives, and feel it my duty to see that my family members are doing the right thing.

I nourish my memories and visit my children, some Baptist, some Catholic, and some who will make their way to Heaven by the skin of their teeth. I watch their children, my precious grandchildren, pray before meals, tell the truth—well, most of the time—and feel guilty when their parents eye them. I chuckle, oddly pleased and content. Ironically, despite my membership in the Methodist church, I have raised good Mennonite children who, in turn, are raising good Mennonite children. I laugh. It seems I can take myself out of the Mennonite community, but I can't take the Mennonite out of me.

In the Order of Age

Phyllis earned a master's degree in English, wrote stories for children, published several games for learners of the English language, and is an accomplished church organist. She married a minister who became the president of the Mennonite Seminary in Fresno, California. She remained a Mennonite.

Grace moved to the southern border of Texas where she and her husband served briefly as missionaries for the Mennonite Brethren Conference before moving to Los Angeles where she worked with children with special needs. She became a Baptist.

Helen died in India at nine months of age, most likely of spinal meningitis.

Paul obtained his doctorate in anthropology and served one term as a Mennonite missionary to India. He taught in several seminaries, although only one was affiliated with the Mennonites. He was a prolific writer on anthropology and missions and spent part of each year teaching in a Bible college in Andhra Pradesh, India.

Elizabeth (Betty) received her doctorate in developmental psychology and taught at Creighton University, a Catholic school, in Omaha, Nebraska. After retiring, she wrote her memoirs, a detailed account of our lives in India. She married a plastic surgeon and became a Presbyterian.

Gwendolyn raised her family before earning her doctorate in educational administration. After serving several years as a school principal, she became a professor at Texas A&M University-Commerce. She is the pianist for the First Methodist Church of Celeste, Texas.

Joanne earned degrees in elementary education, special education, and early childhood. She devoted her career to teaching children with severe and profound handicapping conditions. Her husband taught in the Department of Education at Monmouth College in Illinois. She became a Presbyterian.

Margaret obtained a doctorate in English, and after some years as a university professor and administrator, she earned a degree in nursing. She works as a nurse practitioner in nursing homes, tending to the elderly. She did not remain a Mennonite.

Lois (Loey) earned a masters degree in business administration and worked for IBM for many years. She returned to India to teach and serve as an administrator at Kodaikanal School. She later obtained her doctorate in geography and worked as an administrator of information technology at the University of Montana. She did not remain a Mennonite.

CPSIA information can be obtained at www.ICGtesting.com
Printed in the USA
LVOW132353121012

302673LV00006B/106/P